Parenting Toddlers

Raise a Happy, Social and Confident Child

(Parent's Guide for Children to Teenagers)

William Briggs

Published by Rob Miles

© **William Briggs**

All Rights Reserved

Parenting Toddlers: Raise a Happy, Social and Confident Child (Parent's Guide for Children to Teenagers)

ISBN 9781990084379

All rights reserved. No part of this guide may be reproduced in any form without permission in writing from the publisher except in the case of brief quotations embodied in critical articles or reviews.

Legal & Disclaimer

The information contained in this book is not designed to replace or take the place of any form of medicine or professional medical advice. The information in this book has been provided for educational and entertainment purposes only.

The information contained in this book has been compiled from sources deemed reliable, and it is accurate to the best of the Author's knowledge; however, the Author cannot guarantee its accuracy and validity and cannot be held liable for any errors or omissions. Changes are periodically made to this book. You must consult your doctor or get professional medical advice before using any of the suggested remedies, techniques, or information in this book.

Upon using the information contained in this book, you agree to hold harmless the Author from and against any damages, costs, and expenses, including any legal fees potentially resulting from the application of any of the information provided by this guide. This disclaimer applies to any damages or injury caused by the use and application, whether directly or indirectly, of any advice or information presented, whether for breach of contract, tort, negligence, personal injury, criminal intent, or under any other cause of action.

You agree to accept all risks of using the information presented inside this book. You need to consult a professional medical practitioner in order to ensure you are both able and healthy enough to participate in this program.

Table of Contents

INTRODUCTION 1

CHAPTER 1: THE ALL-STAR LINEUP 2

CHAPTER 2: SINGLE DAD WITH A BABY: THE UNIQUE CHALLENGE OF SINGLE FATHERHOOD 19

CHAPTER 3: "TOGETHER, NOT AGAINST": FEATURES OF RAISING A CHILD WITH A STRONG WILL AND SEARCHING FOR BALANCE 32

CHAPTER 4: ROLES OF PARENTS 37

CHAPTER 5: GETTING TO KNOW YOUR BABY 56

CHAPTER 6: WHAT DO I DO WHEN MY TEENAGER DOES SOMETHING THAT I DISAGREE WITH? 61

CHAPTER 7: YOUR CHILD'S SAFETY 65

CHAPTER 8: LESSON ON CONSISTENCY 81

CHAPTER 9: HOW TO EFFECTIVELY EARN THE 'RESPECT' OF YOUR CHILD 86

CHAPTER 10: CHALLENGE : NEW RESPONSIBILITIES 91

CHAPTER 11: TEEN TO ADULTHOOD 97

CHAPTER 12: BEING THE BEST STEP PARENT POSSIBLE.. 101

CHAPTER 13: BEHAVIOR MANAGEMENT TIPS & TOOLS. 107

CHAPTER 14: DEALING WITH TODDLER TANTRUMS 129

CHAPTER 15: TODDLERS 138

CHAPTER 16: RAISING A HEALTHY CHILD 143

CHAPTER 17: REFUSAL TO EAT AND PLAYING WITH FOOD 146

CHAPTER 18: MOTIVATE AND PRAISE........................... 157

CHAPTER 19: VEHICLE OWNERSHIP 160

CHAPTER 20: EFFECTIVE COMMUNICATION: HOW TO TALK TO AND LISTEN TO YOUR TODDLER............................. 169

CHAPTER 21: IMPORTANT EMERGENCY ITEMS TO INCLUDE WHEN TRAVELING BY RV WITH YOUR BABY.................. 182

CHAPTER 22: SINGLE MOM CHILD CARE OPTIONS - BABY SITTER OR DAY CARE 188

CHAPTER 23: WORK ON YOURSELF 193

CHAPTER 24: STAYING CLOSE TO YOUR DAUGHTER 199

CONCLUSION... 204

Introduction

This book contains proven steps and strategies on how to parent your child with less negativity.

This book includes techniques to help create confident and strong children by turning no into yes and working with your child instead of against. It has communication techniques to build stronger familial bonds between parent and child. The goal of this book is to help parents find new ways to encourage strong emotional growth and problem-solving skills in your child as well as instilling more independence and trust between parent and child.

Thanks again for downloading this book, I hope you enjoy it!

Chapter 1: The All-Star Lineup

Superstar Status: What Difference Does a Dad Make Anyway?

So you're all dressed out in full uniform. You've been at all the practices, even wearing your game face. So, why are you sitting on the bench?

At least in the first few years, a baby's mother is generally the key person in her life. When she is hungry, she wants Mommy. When she is sleepy, your daughter is crying for Mommy. When she is poopie, (thankfully) she wants… yep, none other than her Mommy.

If you ever feel insignificant and perhaps even left out, think again. When you start to wonder, "What difference do I make anyway? When do I get to get in the game?", here is a true story to remind you of the big picture.

It was almost Mother's Day just a few years back. A group of tenderhearted church ladies had recently formed a prison ministry for the nearby men's unit and were excited to pass out some Mother's Day cards for the inmates to send to their mothers. The project was an overwhelming success. In fact, it went so well, the ladies quickly ran out of cards.

Determined not to run out of cards again, the ladies were well-prepared for Father's Day. They went in with a huge sack of cards. No one would be left out. Ironically, only two of the two hundred inmates took cards.

The power of a good father is truly unmatched and it is readily apparent if he is missing. If you doubt that, visit a prison and ask how many inmates had great Dads who were active in their lives when they were in their formative years. Ask them how many currently have the support of their fathers. There will be some, maybe a handful; more times than not, a father figure was missing.

In a 2012 article published by Psychology Today, "Father Absence, Father Deficit, Father Hunger" stated that 85 percent of youth in prison grew up without a father in their lives. The article also cited the fact that the fatherless are more likely to offend and end up incarcerated as adults as well.

The research went on to say that a world of other bad behaviors went hand-in-hand with being raised without a father or father figure. Here are some of the disclosed results of fatherlessness:

71 percent dropped out of school.

The majority struggled with abandonment issues.

An overwhelming number had extremely low self-esteem.

Teen pregnancy was a huge issue.

90 percent of teen runaways were without fathers in their lives.

It seems like a tall order. It's scary thinking that you have such accountability and responsibility. But the fact remains, so you might as well embrace it. Even though you aren't the one carrying the baby in your womb, the part you will play in your little one's life is immense.

Don't worry, your time will come. You'll not only be a starter, you will be a star. As a Dad, you can make a difference. In fact, you make the difference. You will be a game changer!

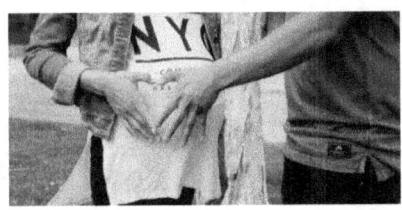

"Honey...we're going to have a baby!"

Finding out you are going to be a Dad is sort of like being drafted into the NFL. You can no doubt remember exactly where you were and what you were doing when you got the news. Maybe the mom-to-be surprised you with the draft papers and you proudly signed on immediately. Or… perhaps not.

No matter how you found out and regardless of whether the pregnancy was one that was meticulously planned (or not), I'm sure you were excited beyond belief… at least eventually. Along with your elation, you probably had a heaping helping of apprehension. Maybe you still do. Don't worry, pre-game jitters are perfectly natural and that is the reason for this book.

Feelings of helplessness are common. As she was hugging the toilet vomiting, you weren't sure what to do. Chances are good that whatever you did (or didn't) do was the wrong thing to do (…or, not do).

"I'm so sorry you feel bad," you may have sympathized. "Can I get you a bowl of ice cream? A pickle?"

Or, perhaps you took the more direct approach. "It's going to be alright, Sweetheart. You'll feel better in about eight months."

If you thought keeping quiet was the best thing to do, I'm sure you found yourself sleeping on the couch.

Regardless, you rapidly learned about some of the discomfort she may experience during her pregnancy:

Nausea (especially in the morning, most notably during the first trimester)

Vomiting

Loss of appetite

Increased appetite (commonly known as "eating for two")

Swollen, tender breasts

Frequent urination

Sleeping too much

Not sleeping enough

Cravings (she will die without a crunchy Frito burrito, or so she thinks)

Muscle aches and pains

Bloating (feeling as if she has swallowed a football)

Gas

Fatigue

Extreme emotions (laughing one minute, crying the next)

All, or at least some, of these "woes" are natural hardships the mother of your child will most likely have to endure. Sometimes (most of the time), there are no right words to say.

What you CAN do is:

Listen. Listening with your heart is one of the single best things you can do for your pregnant partner. Remember what Calvin Coolidge, the 30th President of the United States, said. "It takes a great man to be a good listener."

Affirm her feelings. Affirmation is approving in a positive manner. It's important to affirm the pregnancy, for instance. Saying things like, "You are going to be a great mother because..." while filling in the blank with your own, heartfelt compliment helps make a positive connection while she may not feel well.

Make it a point to affirm her daily if not two or three times a day.

Validate her feelings. When you confirm that her feelings (physical or emotional) are legitimate, you build your communication. Validating doesn't mean you have to agree. According to "Understanding Validation: A Way to Communicate Acceptance" also published by Psychology Today, validating is the recognition and acceptance of another person's feelings.

Be positive. Being "with child" often causes a whirlwind of emotions. Fear, self-doubt and worry may overtake your spouse at times. A positive thought, word or action can turn everything around for her.

Be supportive. Make sure she knows the pregnancy is a "we" thing. Offer to cook dinner, run to the grocery store or clean the house. You can't carry the baby for her, but you can sure make it much easier for her too. Show her she is your queen!

Be sympathetic. Sometimes it's not about knowing how she feels, because you can't possibly know firsthand how it feels to carry a child. It's about imagining yourself being in her position in order to show your concern and an intense sense of caring about what she is going through.

Comfort her. Emotions run rampant during pregnancy. Know that she will most likely experience many realistic and unrealistic fears and well as concerns. "What if there's something wrong with the baby?" or "I'm getting huge. I'm worried I'll have to have a C-section." Your job is to stay calm, cool and collected. Be a help, not a hindrance. Even if her fears are far-fetched, never tell her that. Just ease her mind that everything will be fine; at the same time, don't discount her worries. That is an unforgivable sin.

Go to doctor visits with her. There are few better ways to show your support and enthusiasm than to go to all the doctor visits with your partner. If possible, arrange your work schedule so you can take off for as many as you can. Doctors are used to fathers coming to appointments these days, unlike decades ago when it was rare. You will not only get to hear how mother and baby are doing, but there will most likely be an ultrasound or two you can see firsthand. One ultrasound very well may reveal the gender of your little one. Now that's exciting!

Stay informed. You can impress the mother-to-be when you read about pregnancy and babies. She will feel more at ease, too. There are books, articles and even movies on the subject that will educate you and score you some brownie points with your baby's mamma!

Reassure her. Being pregnant can be uncomfortable, both physically and mentally. Watching her body change is miraculous but at the same time, it's horrifying. Her breasts will be growing, her tummy pouching and she may gain in her thighs and buttocks, too. Reassure her that she looks beautiful "with child." You will want to do this daily because when you feel like you are carrying around a bowling ball, you need to be reminded daily.

Get excited! The more you talk and think about the little bundle of joy you'll be getting, the more excited you will become. There are so many bring things in your future together, be sure to vocalize them. Go shopping for baby clothes, treat her to a new maternity top, go through baby names with your sweetheart… the possibilities are endless. Pregnancy is a journey. Enjoy every step of the way!

Above all, keep your eyes on the prize and encourage your baby's mother to do the same. All the inconveniences of pregnancy (both yours and hers) are a small price to pay for bringing your little human being into the world.

Sex During Pregnancy

First and foremost, at this point, you will be expected to call sex "making love." She will insist on it so don't even wait to be told; it's a given.

Practicing safe sex will now take on a whole new meaning. Now that you and your significant other are expecting, you are (no doubt) wondering if it is safe to have sex. Yes! It is perfectly safe... within reason.

The amniotic sac serves as a really good protector for your little one so she doesn't get bumped or bruised during intercourse. It also serves to keep infection at bay.

Does having sex promote labor? That's an age-old question and the answer is up in the air (no pun intended). If your wife is overdue, some doctors suggest having sex (imagine that!) to help induce labor, but others say it has no effect at all. One thing is certain: if her water has broken, the sac is no longer protecting against things such as infections and it is time to get to the hospital, not to have sex.

You may note that making love during pregnancy is even more rewarding than ever. The two of you share a new bond. You are going to bring a little life into the world all because of a prior love making experience which makes love even sweeter.

Baby Pep Talk

Did you know that at 30 weeks of age (in utero), your baby can actually hear? It's true. And when your baby is born, he'll recognize your voice, too.

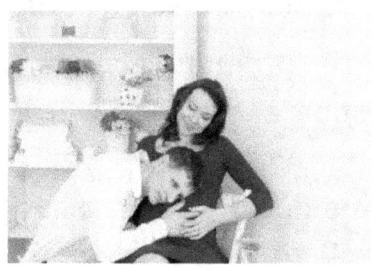

Not only is talking to your belly bump an absolutely awesome way to bond, it helps your baby's development. Here are some additional ways it works.

Auditory Stimulation. As early as 14 weeks, your little one's auditory system begins to develop. Talking and even singing to her helps ensure her development is right on key.

Brain Development. The more your baby is exposed to sounds (and sights later), the more her brain will pick up to process. Experts say that it is good for a baby's brain development to hear both the mother and the father's voice pitches.

Security. Your baby will feel safe and secure when you talk to her. You can imagine how comforting it would be.

Family Ties. Not only will you and your baby bundle bond, talking to your baby bump strengthens ties between you and your baby's Momma as well.

Here are some tips for talking to your bump:

Tip #1	If you know what you baby's name will be, use his name when you talk.

Tip #2	Don't limit yourself to talking, you can also sing. Even if you aren't the greatest singer, don't worry. Your baby will not care.
Tip#3	Try reciting poems and nursery rhymes too.
Tip#4	If you have other children, why not let them join in some great sibling bonding? Let them have a turn singing or talking to the baby. One of the cutest things ever was when my friend told me her youngest boy was repetitively telling the baby (bump) "Knock-Knock" jokes. I was there when the baby was born and was astonished when the little brother spoke and the baby looked around for him. There was no denying that she recognized the familiar voice.

Learn the Lingo

First Trimester: Weeks 1-12 of pregnancy

Second Trimester: Weeks 13 to 27

Third Trimester: Week 28 to birth

Term: The length of pregnancy, which is generally 40 weeks

Fetus: The baby before birth

Gynecologist: A doctor (who you will probably get to know on first name basis before all is said and done), also known as a female reproduction system physician or an OBGYN (because the OB stands for obstetrician, the part of the doctor's learning that's specifically for babies).

Nursery: What you will paint at least once, where you will put the baby furniture you assemble and later where you will put the baby... sometimes.

Chapter Takeaways

It is very normal to be both happy and scared to death when you find out you are going to be a Dad.

Your baby's Mom will most likely have some pregnancy symptoms, such as morning sickness.

You can be a great help to her by doing things around the house, reading about pregnancy as well as childbirth and by being sympathetic.

Talking to your baby while he is in his Mommy's tummy is an awesome way to bond and is great for his brain development as well.

The duration of pregnancy is generally 40 weeks and is divided into three trimesters.

Chapter 2: Single Dad With A Baby: The Unique Challenge Of Single Fatherhood

Everyone knows that raising a child is not easy even with both parents around. Everyone knows that raising a child as a single mom is even tougher. But only a few realize that raising a child as a single dad can be a nightmare.

For example, very few realize that juggling between work and caregiving to a child less than one year old is one of the toughest things for single dads. Striking a balance between his work and child care is the first major challenge single dads have to hurdle because it is simply impossible to accomplish without much sacrifice.

Single Dad with a baby is a major challenge.

If you are a single dad with a good paying job, chances are your work comes with inflexible hours and even requires doing some time after work - which means you will hardly have time to take care of your baby. Of course there are day-care and babysitting options you can consider but if you make use of any of these options, you will find yourself always rushing home to get to the baby before the time is up.

Besides, day care is going to cost you a fortune. The average cost of day care center for infants and toddlers range from $4,550 per year (in Mississippi) to $18,750 per year (in Massachusetts). Without savings and healthcare benefits you will surely be a lame duck. Even the low end range of the day care costs amounts to more than 10% of the average income of single dads. According to the Department of Health and Human Services parents should not be spending more than 10% of their income for day care alone - or they won't be able to save enough for the child's college education. (You're lucky if the company you are working with is one of those which shoulders part of the day care expenses of their working single parent employees.)

If you have day care, getting home after picking up the baby from the center is not the end of the day for you. It is only the beginning of your daily single dad ordeal so expect more single daddy tasks ahead.

You have to wash, feed, and play with the baby before preparing him for bed. After putting the baby to sleep, you will have to clean and sanitize the baby bottles, tidy the house, do the laundry, and oh, you have to eat too so you need to do some cooking – and don't forget you have to wash the dishes afterwards.

By the time you hit the sack, you will probably be too exhausted and may fall asleep almost immediately. Midway through the night, you may have to wake up to change the baby's diapers and give him a fresh bottle of milk. You also need to get up early because usually babies are up early. That means you have to force yourself out of bed no matter how lacking in sleep and how tired you were the day and the night before.

The next day won't be any different from yesterday. After feeding, cleaning, and dressing up the baby, you will have to prepare the baby's bag of goodies and fill it with enough diapers, wipes, extra clothes, and feeding bottles that will last for the day before bringing him to the day care center again for the new day. Afterwards, you have to prepare yourself for work. Forget about breakfast – you can grab some on your way to the office. While at work, you may have to call the center to check on how your baby is doing. Weekends are not going to be any different too because it will have to be with the baby all day and all night long.

You have to realize that single dads with babies to take care of are under a lot of pressure and stress. Single parent burnout is not uncommon. If you happen to be a single dad, you have to realize that you need to be mentally, financially, and physically prepared to meet up to the many grueling challenges of single fatherhood. There won't be any ifs or buts and there is no reasoning your way out of any of it. You have to meet the challenges squarely because your own child's future is what is at stake. Remember, momentary negligence can cost you your child's good future.

So, how do other single dads cope with this challenge?

Some dads quit their regular jobs altogether to spend more time with their babies. They look for other jobs with more flexible hours or settle for some stay-at-home jobs. This often means taking a huge pay cut which will also (unfortunately) mean having less money for health care. It is the only option if they want to spend more time with the baby or avoid paying for expensive day care expenses.

This is probably one of the reasons why the average income of single dad households in the country is comparatively low - hovering just a little bit above the poverty line. This is something that must be viewed with utmost concern by every single dad because if a child grows up in poverty or wanting in his basic needs, he is likely to have personality and behavioral problems in the future.

It is not time to throw in the towel though. If your current salary can't get your baby into day care what you can do is to establish your own support network. Sign up your parents, your aunt or uncle, your siblings, your cousins, or any of your close friends and relatives whom you can call at a moment's notice to take care of the baby. Try your faith community members too. They may also be able to help you.

Explain your predicament and get their pledges to help you. Put all the names and numbers of all those who agreed to help in a notebook and place the notebook somewhere that is easily accessible. Make sure you separate those who pledged to help you on a regular basis and try to make a schedule for them. The rest will be your alternates – pitching in case the regulars will have some unexpected activities to attend to. The larger your support network is, the less worries you will have.

Knowing you have someone you can safely leave your baby with (if the day care option is not feasible) will give you peace of mind and allow you to take care of the baby without leaving your regular work. Just don't make a mistake of leaving the baby with someone you hardly know.

When the baby won't stop crying

Another one of the most taxing tasks single dads with babies have to face is how to stop the baby from crying. A baby crying non-stop can drive people nuts, especially if they haven't had a wink of sleep and have to report for work early the next day.

The first thing you need to know about babies crying is they don't cry without a reason. They cry because they are upset with something. And, they won't stop unless the discomfort brought by whatever it is that upsets them is gone. The only problem is they can't speak to tell you exactly what's troubling them. You can only try to guess the reason why the baby is upset. Even the most experienced and the most knowledgeable parent have difficulty in finding out why babies cry - so this is going to be another tough one for the single dad.

Here are some secrets you can try to help you find out why the baby is upset:

Check the baby's diaper. A wet diaper irritates the baby's skin and makes him uncomfortable. Change the diaper immediately. If the diaper is dry look for signs of diaper rash like redness or swelling around the diaper area. If the baby has diaper rash then stop using disposable diapers. Use cotton cloth diapers instead but make sure you coat the affected area with diaper rash ointment first before you put on the cotton diaper.

The baby may be hungry. Try stroking your baby's cheek slowly with hand. If he turns his head towards your hand, it means he is hungry. Another secret to find out if the baby is hungry is to touch gently the soft spot on top of your baby's head. It is called the anterior fontanel. If it is depressed, that means the baby is hungry. Don't worry it won't do the baby any harm if you touch his soft spot gently with your fingers. The milk you are giving may no longer be enough. So consult your pediatrician – it may be time to give your baby some baby cereals.

The baby may be having gas pains. They may have taken a lot of air while feeding or while crying. You can help him work the gas out by burping him. Another way is to lie him on his back, hold his legs, and move the legs gently in circular motions like he is pedaling a bicycle. Don't attempt to give him any medication unless his doctor says so.

The baby just wants to be cuddled. Your baby may want to sense your presence, hear your voice or listen to your heartbeat. This is what he was used to while inside his mother's womb. Swaddle him and hold him close to your chest. Try to simulate the environment he was in while inside the womb.

The baby may be over-stimulated. Babies get stimulated by everything around him like the noise, the lights, or being passed from one person to another. His immediate environment is part of his learning process. However, there are times when he may have had too much exposure and cries out loud to tell you he needs a break. Again, swaddle him and keep him close to your chest. This will give him warmth and a feeling of security.

The baby may be running a fever. Try touching the baby's forehead with your cheek. If his forehead is hotter than usual then get a thermometer and get an accurate reading of his temperature. If it is over 380 C, then he has a fever. It is a sign that he is coming down with something. Take the baby in a cooler room and take off any thick clothing. Allow the baby to cool down for a while. You can put a damp cloth on his forehead to help lower his temperature. If the fever last for more than one day, take him to the doctor immediately.

Summing it up, there are basically 3 things you need to check first to find out why the baby is crying – his diaper, an empty stomach, or a fever. If none of these is a problem then your guess is as good as mine. But don't despair because there are a lot of other things you can do to pacify the baby even if you have failed to identify the reason why he is upset.

Here are some ways to calm the baby and stop them from crying even if you don't why he is upset:

Give the baby a pacifier to suck. Sucking on to something calms down the baby and relaxes his stomach. It also steadies his heartbeat.

Swaddle and snuggle him. Babies are longing for the warmth and security of his mother's womb. So wrap the baby snuggly in a blanket and hold him close to your chest. This simulates the feeling of being in his mother's womb again.

Try to play some music or sing a lullaby and dance while holding the baby. This may be an old trick but it still works for some babies today.

Hold him close to a source of 'white noise' - like the sound of a washing machine or a vacuum cleaner. Their sounds mimic the constant buzzing sounds of body movements the baby used to hear when he was still in his mother's womb. This trick can be soothing to babies and it is worth giving it a try.

Bring the baby outside or simply open the door for some fresh air. Some babies stop crying as soon as you open the door or step outside the house.

Give the baby a gentle massage. Babies love to be touched. Giving him a soothing, slow, and gentle massage brings comfort to him.

Don't give up easily. The crying and the screaming is not going to last forever so don't lose your nuts and bolts. Besides, as the baby grows older the crying and the screaming is going to subside.

Chapter 3: "Together, Not Against":

Features Of Raising A Child With A Strong Will And Searching For Balance

Now that you know your child's more difficult traits are also his biggest gifts, you must learn how to work with him rather than against him. Allow him to grow his traits and become the person he was born to be without going crazy or feeling like you have no control.

The first key is to always remain calm. Raising your voice or resorting to physical punishments is a good way to alienate your child and sever the bond that is so crucial between parent and child. You will also get into a shouting match that will benefit no one and lead nowhere.

The second key is to establish boundaries and discipline that is guaranteed to happen when he breaks these boundaries. A good example is a rule about not getting your own cookies out of the jar without asking for permission. If your child breaks this rule, then he is not allowed cookies for the rest of the day. Keep the punishments consistent so your child learns that breaking the rules gets him nowhere with you. Realize that your child will repeatedly test these boundaries. This is just his way of exploring how the world works and what loopholes he can find. It is a useful skill later in life – though it is trying now at this time.

The third key is to remember that your child strongly identifies with you. His ego is closely tied with your opinion of him and he wants your praise. If he breaks the rules, then he faces the consequences you have clearly laid out. But you should never insult his personality or tell him that he is a bad child. It is far more effective to show him love and give him positive reinforcement when you notice that he is engaging in good behaviors. This encourages him to be good more often than bad.

The final, and perhaps most important, key is to never take things personally with a child like this. Your strong-willed child will constantly be studying you and testing you. He is probing for ways to disrupt the status quo and get what he wants. This is the stubbornness, confidence, and creativity all at play. Obviously, this can be quite infuriating. But you can keep it from becoming negative by never letting it turn into a fight. Don't take this personally – he is not doing it to attack or provoke you deliberately. He is simply feeling out the world, and you are the best model for him to test. Use a reasonable attitude and tell him that your rules are firm. Explain how the world works using a reasonable tone and solid examples. In this way, you turn his traits into strengths rather than points of contention.

It is important to understand that life is permanently changed with the entry of this child. You will grow as a person as you learn infinite patience and self-control. It is not always easy or fun. You will even fail at times. But the end result is extremely rewarding. Every day is a new opportunity for you to improve yourself, and your child will provide the curriculum for your self-growth. Become focused on relaxing, being patient, and solving problems without needless anger or emotion. Learn to use empathy and understanding at all times and try to approach things from your child's point of view. Finally, stop taking things personally and acting out if provoked. Taking a deep breath and learning to go with the flow is instrumental in handling a strong-willed child.

One thing that really helps is to appreciate the good time and easy days. Celebrate these times with your child. Try to do lots of bonding activities to have fun, instead of simply enforcing rules. You are more to your child than a rule enforcer. Having fun distracts him from being unruly and helps you appreciate your bond rather than becoming frustrated or bitter. When he behaves, consider a pizza party or a trip to a playground a great reward to celebrate his accomplishment and strengthen your bond together.

Chapter 4: Roles Of Parents

The most powerful desire or drive in a man is often his physiological need to fulfill the act of procreation.

Modern society and families have changed drastically from previous generations. The new attitude towards sex (right or wrong) has led to an increase in the number of unplanned pregnancies.

Anyone can be a sperm-donor and be a biological father of a child, but it takes more to be a dad. It takes a lot more also to be a mom than carrying a child for nine months.

We often assume parenting should come automatically and that we will be better parents than the parents that raised us. Relationships are like rose gardens when well-kept they are beautiful. But if we leave our relationships un-kept we will end up with dysfunctional relationships that bring us nothing but stress.

Roles that a parent must focus on

There are six main roles that a parent must focus on: Love, Guidance, Provision, Security, Friendship, and Development.

Each child is different, and some children need more attention than others, especially strong-willed children, but we must fulfill our role as parents regardless of the difficulty. One thing all parents must learn is that having children is undoubtedly a life-changing event.

No matter how many children we have, each child is different and unique with a different set of challenges.

LOVE

Some parents believe that loving a child will come easy and for the most part it does. However, there are moments when love becomes strained, and tempers flare. Maybe the child is not on your schedule and not allowing you to sleep (which happens the first few months of life).

Strong-willed children may often test the boundaries of love. They may often leave you exhausted and even depressed with their antics. If you are at your wits end, you are not alone. The trick is to get help.

When you become challenged in raising a strong-willed child, try and get help. If you have a partner, you can both take turns in dealing with your difficult child. If you are a single parent, you may need to reach out for assistance, in raising the child, from siblings or the grandparents but don't try and do it alone.

Even when you are stressed-out from parenting, you still have a responsibility to love the child. If you start to feel the strain, seek help and try to take a break if you can.

But when we talk about love in relationships, we are not just talking exclusively about some sense of mutual endearment or fondness.

Parenting a strong-willed child will require what is referred to as "tough love." As children learn about the world they live in they will often do make choices they shouldn't. As parents if we love our children then we must encourage them to do what's right. Sometimes we have a misplaced sense of what love is in parenting and we focus too much on endearment in times when we are required to show tough love.

When we focus on being liked or loved by our children rather than on encouraging them to do what's right for their good, then it's not them that we love but ourselves.

You must ask yourself are you sacrificing their long-term fulfillment and happiness in life, for your short-term sense of peace and endearment.

When your child takes a jar of jam from the supermarket aisle and smashes it on the floor because you refused to buy a toy for them, what do you do?

However, you choose to correct the behavior is down to you, but you must correct this behavior. If we willingly allow them to develop a sense of self-entitlement and lack of respect for authority, we are not showing love, as we are facilitating and encouraging behavior that will prevent them from developing into well-rounded adults.

Some parents result to yelling to correct bad behavior. But shouting does not help at any stage during development. When tempers flare, and words are spouted out, there is no telling the damage those words can cause.

Although the child does need to understand that what they just did is wrong, it does not help getting angry. As parents especially with strong-willed children we must be in control of our emotions at all times.

Sometimes it might be better to leave the child if possible and allow things to cool down, and for clear heads to prevail before dealing with the situation.

Many parents get upset with toddlers who simply don't know any better because they have not learned the difference between right and wrong. This lack of emotional control will only exacerbate the situation.

Love is the ability to look past mistakes and guide your kid regardless of the emotional toll of doing so.

Love is tender and gentle even when gum gets stuck in their hair, and things are a bit messy. They have to learn somehow and giving a child the proper space to learn makes a world of difference. Not only does it allow for them to explore on their terms and test new things, but it also helps the parents keep their cool during playtime.

When counseling parents, I often tell them, love is the most powerful weapon you have as a parent. I have seen so many children's lives be transformed when the parent simply starts to foster a greater sense of love in the home. When you create an environment of love, parenting will become easier.

You will feel a sense of accomplishment when you ask you strong-willed child to do something, and they obey not because they are scared, but because they love you and want to make you happy.

A practical example I can give you on this is how I taught my child to clean her room. I remember the frustration of coming home and seeing the room looking like a bomb was set off. As I said, previously yelling doesn't always work with strong-willed children, so I tried a different approach.

I said to my then 5-year-old "Your room is messy again, should we clean it up together before we make your bedtime hot chocolate?"

Then I proceeded to help clear up and turned it into a fun game. Soon she enjoyed clearing up so much she would ask if I wanted to help her clean-up. A few months after that she would clean up all by herself and then shout "Mom…….dad, my room is clean… Can I have my cocoa now?"

But it gets better after 6 months of her new found sense of accomplishment tidying up her room she started to observe when things were untidy in the house and ask why we hadn't cleaned up, mimicking my voice as best as she could.

The morale of the story is once I replaced frustration with love I was able to see things more objectively and help correct the undesirable behavior. I have seen others get the same results by replacing yelling with patience and love.

GUIDANCE

It is often said the first five years are the most formative of a child's life. It is the parent's responsibility to teach them and build up the child emotionally. Praise the child when they have done a good deed and correct them when they have done something not so nice or pleasant.

Guidance is more than teaching extremes or polar ends of morality. Guidance is about helping them develop a moral compass, direction and the noble traits and qualities we want them to have in life without indoctrinating them and stealing their ability to come to their own conclusions.

A child does not understand the word "no" and unfortunately that one particular word is the most familiar word a child will hear growing up.

During a child's exploration, a parent may look over to discover little Jane is digging in the dirt of a flowerpot. The mess, of course, is easy to fix, and the enjoyment of the soft squishy dirt between the fingers is new. However, it is the mess not the action, that causes a resentful "NO!" from the parent. It is not as if the parent doesn't want Jane to play in the dirt; it is the mess she is causing.

The child may not see the difference in playing with this sandbox inside the house, to playing with it outside. Yet, many parents may flare up and even spank the child as they lose emotional control. Understanding that your child does not understand the difference and taking the time to explain may be more beneficial than shouting at them in anger.

Many parents source of frustration, stems from them repeating their bad parenting habits and expecting different results. Yelling and spanking are not always effective, and can serve to only re-enforce your child's strong will.

In situations like above, it would be wiser to remove the child to the sandbox outside and explain the difference. Redirection is one form of guidance. Although it is simple to remove the child and explain the difference between the sandbox and the flowerpot, there will be times when it is not so easy.

Skip ahead a few years later and Jane is now a teen. When strong-willed children become teenagers, it often presents a challenging time to parents. The cute naughty strong-willed child is now at the stage where peer pressure competes with instructions and guidance.

Jane's new peers have the power to influence her decisions. During this stage, some parents think that they can guide the child by ruling with an iron fist.

If Jane knows the reaction from her parents will be one of anger, it is possible, that she will rebel just to get a rise out of her parents, as she figures out there are no longer any consequences to bad behavior. If Jane knows that her parents are not easily manipulated emotionally, she might not be so tempted to try to behave poorly to get a reaction.

In dealing with strong-willed teens, you must objectively determine the cause of bad behavior. Are they behaving poorly to get a reaction or are they just trying to fit in with the wrong crowd?

The answer to the above question should take precedence in how you decide to tackle the situation.

The biggest problem during this time is the parent's belief that their words no longer hold any weight. The fact is, they do. Even if the child seems distant and unresponsive to that talk on sexual education, that is so uncomfortable for the parent, the child is listening. Everything is a learning experience, and no one knows everything and things are constantly changing. If that drug speech is boring, find a way to spruce it up or even a movie. Media is a great mediator for parents these days. Taking the mystery out of something like sex or drugs makes it less appealing. But the parent must make time for the child for them to seize the moment and guide them onto the right path. Time is one thing that everyone seems to be short of, which is why it is important to provide the time your child needs. As a parent, it is imperative to put the child's needs above your own.

PROVISION

Providing for young ones is an area historically parents have thrived in, we provide clothes, food, water, housing, education, to name a few.

However, in us trying to provide we can often neglect the other aspects of parenting. Some parents work 60, 70, 80+ hours a week all in the name of providing a better life for the family. However, often we can fail to get the balance right and miss out on what is critical in life.

We may provide our children million dollar mansions and servants at their disposal. But what is the point if we are not around to be a part of their formative years?

Billionaires like Warren Buffet and Carlos Slim often chose quieter less privileged lives, so their children grow up balanced.

Studies show that giving your child everything they want may destroy them. If you can afford to buy your teen son a supercar for his eighteenth birthday, what values do you think you are instilling in him?

The fortunes we try so hard to amass and pass on are often squandered within two generations as we often pass on money but not the qualities and traits of wealth creation like hard work and responsibility that got us our success.

Our role is to provide them the basics of what they need to flourish, but not each and every desire. There is nothing wrong with showering our children with expensive gifts as long as in exchange the child is learning something valuable.

I remember counseling a parent who spoiled her teen so bad that her daughter had the latest Smartphone on the market each year at the cost of over a thousand dollars. The child was doing poorly in school and had no sense of responsibility, yet her parents rewarded her bad behavior by giving in to her every demand.

I often tell parents, use treats and gifts as an incentive to build character. Surprise them with what they want when they perform exceptionally well. But also, teach them to do well for doing good sake.

Material sustenance is not the only thing we need to provide.

As parents of strong-willed children, one of the things you are required to provide your child is time.

Many times we fall into the trap of thinking money can substitute for time. Sub-consciously we realize that maybe we haven't spent as much time as we should have with our children, and we tend to over-compensate with lavish gifts.

It is the little things that count. From the notes left in the lunch box to encourage the child to do well on a test and to show support. To the text messages when they forgot to check in after school.

Parenting requires time spent preparing the child for their future, and to build a strong support group.

Even if dad works late to pay the bills, that don't mean that is where his role ends. Parenting is the time spent after the daily routine of work and chores. That is why it is the little things that matter the most.

Building up a person is a full-time job in itself. Self-doubt can creep in at any time which can cause fear. It is the parent's job to look under the bed at night to make sure there are no monsters. Or even praise the child for the raise they received from work. Being involved in a child's life does not mean one has to be overbearing or nosy. It means that when the child picks up the phone to talk, the parent listens. There are so many parents in this world that are so focused on their lives and list of to-dos that they miss their chance to provide for their child.

SECURITY

One of the most important roles of a parent is to provide security. As our children are developing, it is our duty to not only guide them but also to protect them from harm. There are many dangers in the world they are growing up in particularly those brought about by the very choices our children may make.

But regardless of the source of danger, it is the parent's duty as a responsible adult to stand up for their child. If the child is bullied at school or if the child feels pinned against various odds, it is the parent's job to step up and fight for their child. Many parents these days leave the child to battle on their own with the mentality of the survival of the fittest. This mentality, however, may work in nature but as humans, this concept is flawed. To build trust with a child, the parent must prove to the child that they will fight for them.

It is, however, the parent's responsibility to provide the child with a safe environment free from verbal, emotional and physical abuse. Even if that does mean taking away a new phone so that the texts stop, or the computer, so the hate mail ends.

FRIENDSHIP

Inwardly most parents desire to be best friends with their kids. At one point in their lives we may have been the center of their world, but as time goes on kids will often become disinterested in their parents.

This is why it is important where possible to foster friendship with our children at an early age. But friendship with our children should not be used as an emotional crutch if we are unfulfilled in our own lives.

Becoming friends with our kids is about fostering a loving relationship, where the child knows we are their parent but still feels they can talk to us, hang out with us or share with us without always having the obstacle of the typically defined role of parenthood.

Chapter 5: Getting To Know Your Baby

Welcome to motherhood! Your 9 month pregnancy may have ended, but it also signals the start of a more exciting journey. You walk back into your home with a newborn baby in your arms and all you want to do is to stare at your little angel. Then suddenly the question dawns on you and your partner, what do you do now?

• Communicate – One of the first things you would want to do is to understand what your newborn wants. Pay close attention because babies are born with the urge to communicate with you and every move they make means something. Observe how they react to your touch – the way you hold them, they way you dress them, the way you feed them. This way you'll learn more about your baby and your baby will learn more from you too.

- Respond quickly – This is a phase where your baby is still developing his sense of trust. The stress of the baby soon declines when he builds confidence that you are always there and that you understand what he needs.

- Learn from all the crying – A crying baby always brings panic among new moms. What does my baby want? She's been crying the whole night what else do I need to do? Instead of going nuts and finding yourself in the verge of your own tears, try to understand what the variations of his tears mean.

The cry: starts mild, intermittent, and breathy, building up to a wail. Abruptly stops when distracted. Can last for an hour.

What it really means: This is the most common cry, but can be consoled. Hold the baby in his favorite position; get rid of anything that may annoy him, sooth the baby with your touch. Come up with all tactics, the key is to make the baby feel more comfortable

The cry: Whimpering, urgent and panicked cry with flailing or legs up.

What it really means: It may be indigestion, or maybe the baby has swallowed air or needs a burp.

The cry: Open mouthed wail accompanied with rubbing of eyes

What it really means: The little one is tired. Try swaddling with a cloth or bring him to a dark room with soothing music to calm him down and induce sleep. This is also a great opportunity to bond by singing to him until Sandman comes.

The cry: A startled pause followed by a high-pitched wail.

What it really means: Some babies get startled easily, or do not like to get separated from their moms. This is one of the easier to address as it can be easily consoled with a comforting caress and a hug.

The cry: Repeated nyah-nyah cries, that build up in volume.

What it really means: Especially if it has been 4 hours since their last feeding, the baby is most likely hungry.

When your child is inconsolable for extended hours or the wailing is violently different, check to see if the baby is sick or if something is really wrong. Other babies on the other hand just need to be left alone crying for some time before they are able to sleep. Some babies cry more than others, but it doesn't mean that you are a bad parent. The key is to really focus on the child and try to recognize what he/she is trying to tell you. Trust your maternal instincts, God gave them for a reason.

• The power of your touch – Being newborns, babies will most respond to touch and sound. Skin to skin contact is very important as it calms down the child and helps develop their emotional security. It's good for you too, as direct contact with your child decreases stress and tendency of the parent to get depressed.

• Music – Music is truly the universal language. It speaks to your babies too. It helps soothe and relax them, and helps to develop their brains. Studies show that classical music helps to develop the parts of their brain that are used for spatial reasoning. The best music though is the sound of your voice singing to your baby before they sleep, it further develops the maternal bond and helps baby to learn language early.

• Feeding – solid food is discouraged until 6 months, and one of the best things you can do for your baby is to breastfeed. The reason why most women could not breastfeed is that it can get terribly hard and painful. Get yourself a breastfeeding guide to learn the various techniques and tips. When you have gotten over the trial and error days, breastfeeding will be one of the most rewarding activities you could experience. Not only does it benefit the child, but it's also great for you and your well-being!

Chapter 6: What Do I Do When My Teenager Does Something That I Disagree With?

This is a difficult question, because many of us will have the initial reaction of just getting upset and angry, because we think that those emotions are going to push our teenagers to do what we want them to do. But the issue is, here, that too many parents are rude and even mean to their teenagers when they do something wrong. This reaction is understandable, but there are a lot of ways that you can deal with it that will help you to stay relatable to your teenager without being walked all over.

First, you may need to consider taking a timeout in order to collect your thoughts. Most arguments occur because one or both parties are being defensive and/or reactionary, instead of thinking through what they're saying. Emotions can get in the way of civil conversation, and that will make the entire process of reconciliation and figuring out how to resolve the issue in a healthy way, near impossible.

After that, make sure that you talk in a place that is safe for both of you. If you have to, go out and get something to eat or drink in order to neutralize the air for both of you (and, as you would expect, you're less likely to argue or yell when you're in a public area. Food and drink are soothing to most people, and can be a good starting point if you're looking for a commonality. As we mentioned in the first section on this book, food is a good conversation starter, too.

If you are 'blowing up' at each other too often, you may want to sit down with someone that you trust that is not part of your family. Whether that's a family friend, a clergy member, a mentor or youth leader, or even a therapist, having a neutral party available when you talk things out can help ease the stress on both of you. A third party can also help both of you try to understand what the other is saying and thinking.

What should you be exploring in these conversations? Here are some talking points that you may want to explore during your initial conversation.

- You need to explain what your reaction was to their action, belief, or statement, and why you reacted that way. Use "I" statements; that way, your teenager doesn't feel like they have to defend themselves. It opens the way for actual conversation to occur.

- Ask them why they made the decision that they made. Don't be accusatory; let them know that you love them no matter their reasoning behind their actions. Instead, inquire gently, like asking "What prompted you to make that decision?" or even something more vague, like "What are your thoughts about this whole thing?"

- Just listen! One thing that many parents don't do well is listening. Show that you're genuinely interested by making eye contact, repeating what they tell you to show that you're trying to understand, and using other forms of body language that express interest.

By following all of the above patterns and ideas, it will be much easier for you to determine what is going on between the two of you. It can reduce a lot of stress during the conversation. There will, of course, still be times that you disagree. But by following these simple tips, you can make those disagreements a lot less explosive.

Chapter 7: Your Child's Safety

Childproofing Your Home

Parents suffer immense distress when their child is seriously injured in the comfort of their own home. A seemingly safe haven is actually full of hidden dangers. Childproofing becomes an essential element in providing protection for both your child and your property. Like all parents, you naturally want to provide the best possible environment for your toddler, avoiding the unnecessary tumbles, bumps, fractures and other serious injuries that can be avoided by understanding potential dangers and taking the necessary measures to avoid them. Here are some key safety points when childproofing your home:

Important Safety Measures

• Always keep a list of all emergency phone numbers within easy reach near the phone.

• Purchase and install child resistant locks and latches on drawers and cupboards, especially those that contain poisonous and dangerous substances and sharp objects. All cleaning chemicals and products should be kept out of sight and out of reach.

• Always keep a first aid kit in your car and in your home. Parents should also learn CPR and other basic first aid.

• Safety gates should be installed to block stairs, kitchen, steps and other areas that should not be accessed by toddlers unsupervised.

• Use safety plugs installed in unused electrical sockets.

• If your child also spends a lot of time in their grandparent's house or other areas, it should also be sufficiently childproofed.

Floors

• Keep floors clean from any liquid spills to avoid slips

- Clear floors of any small objects that could easily be swallowed
- If you have hard floor surfaces such as tiles and polished floorboards, do not allow your toddler to walk around wearing socks.

Dining Area and Lounge

- Install corner protectors on furniture pieces with hard edges.
- Seal off stairs and steps using safety gates.
- Use tablemats instead of tablecloths, which can be easily pulled down by toddlers.
- Do not leave any hot drink or soup unattended, where they can be easily reached.
- Do not place furniture near any balcony railings and windows.
- Install fireguard on heather and fireplace, as open fires easily attract kids.

- Ensure television and stereo sets are firmly secured.

Kitchen, Bathroom and Laundry

- Install safety gates on areas you don't want your child to access.

- When cooking and preparing food, make sure your child is in a high chair or on the playpen so they will not get in your way.

- Install locks on fridge doors and ovens, ensuring all appliance cords are out of reach.

- Saucepan handles should always be turned inwards so it cannot be easily grabbed.

- Use form-fitting lids on washing buckets, baths and toilets. Do not leave your toddler unsupervised near water.

- Always test the water temperature. Taps can also be fitted valves to control water temperature.

- When ironing clothes, place your toddler in a playpen and out of harm's way.

Bedrooms

• Never place a baby on high surfaces and leave him unattended.

• Sleeping cots should be placed away from heaters, cords, blinds and windows.

• When staying in your room, make sure perfumes and jewelry items are out of reach, especially those that can be easily swallowed.

• Keep dry cleaning bags out of reach as it presents suffocation risks.

Pets

• If you have pets around the house, do not leave them around children without adult supervision. Toddlers tend to prod and poke animals, which can trigger animal aggression.

• Before purchasing a pet, consult a veterinarian or pet breeder to determine which particular breed of cat or dog will best suit your family.

Stranger Danger: Streetproofing Your Toddler

When we teach children the inherent dangers of the outside world, we often remind them not to talk to strangers. But is it enough? Unfortunately, the world is one big scary place and some people like to prey on children. Stranger danger is one important issue that every parent must address. However, streetproofing your child is not a one-time session, but will require an ongoing communication.

First, how do you define "strangers"?

When teaching your child about stranger danger, it is important to properly define who should be labeled as strangers. Of course, not all people that are not known to them pose danger. Your toddler needs to understand the difference between "good strangers" and "bad strangers" in an overly simplistic way that kids can understand.

It is also important for your child to know where and whom they can turn to when lost or when they feel scared. Examples for "good' strangers include security guards, teachers, police officers and store clerks. Let your toddler understand that he can turn to the "good" strangers for help and assistance.

When "bad" strangers approach by luring or physically pulling them away, train your kids to know what to do and get attention of other adults by making enough noise. Here are some important pointers and strategies to teach your child about stranger danger:

• Teach your child to memorize his parent's name, address and phone number.

• Introduce the buddy system—never allow them to walk alone without any companion.

• Teach your child not to talk to strangers or approach a stranger in a motor vehicle and not to accept any candy or other items from a stranger.

• Teach your child some defense mechanisms such as kicking, biting and screaming when a stranger grabs him forcibly.

When teaching your kids about stranger danger, role-playing scenarios have been known to be highly effective.

What is stranger anxiety?

When toddlers are introduced to new people, they do not only meet them but also remember them. A child's capacity to recognize people he knows and those he doesn't know grows as he ages and may instinctively start to fear people he does not recognize, especially people who look different. Some toddlers skip this particular behavior altogether.

How to address stranger anxiety?

The most effective way to cure stranger anxiety or shyness is to regularly expose your toddler to new people. Take them to public places such as the park or grocery store, where he can freely choose to be with you or mingle with other people. You can then start to introduce your toddler to new people. If your child still resists or prefers to be glued to you, allow him to simply observe people from the safety of mom or dad. It will also help to warn people not to be overly pushy with your child. Typically, stranger anxiety will eventually go away on its own over a period of time. Rest assured that this is not an indication that your child will have difficulty socializing or making friends in the future. Just give him ample time to adjust.

What Parents Need to Know about Lead Poisoning

Lead poisoning typically occurs when a person absorbs, inhales or swallows lead in any form. For children in particular, lead poisoning can cause significant damage to the nerves and brain as well as other major parts of the body. Chronic lead poisoning is more common among children, where they ingest small amounts of lead over a longer period of time. This can often result to learning disabilities, mental retardation and behavioral problems. At extremely high levels, lead poisoning can cause coma and even death.

Possible Causes

Before it was discovered to be harmful, lead was widely used in gasoline, paint and other consumer products. Here are some possible sources of lead that every parent should know about:

• Lead-based Paint—one of the most common sources of lead exposures among preschoolers. Watch out for paint chips on old buildings and painted surfaces like windowsills.

• Dust and Soil—both can be contaminated by past emissions of leaded gasoline and old paint.

• Drinking Water—old lead water pipes, which are common in old homes, which are built before 1930.

• Jobs and Hobbies—there are a number of activities that may expose you and your child to lead such as pottery making, refinishing furniture pieces, working on stained glass and DIY home repairs.

Symptoms

- Hyperactivity or fatigue
- Unexplained irritability
- Reduced attention span
- Loss of appetite
- Aggressive behavior
- Unexplained weight loss
- Vomiting and headache
- Constipation
- Lack of motor control and balance

Prevention

When dealing with lead, the best form of intervention is prevention. Toddler caretakers should be properly educated on the risks of lead poisoning and how to avoid it. It is important not to allow toddlers to chew on non-food items.

Houses that are near freeways and industrial factories have higher risk exposure to lead. It is important for parents to have their children tested and screened for lead contamination. For homes found to have lead, residential owners have two options: complete lead removal conducted by experts or making the home lead-safe. The former is more expensive and will require property owners to vacate to a temporary home while lead removal is underway. The second option does not render the home lead-free, but instead covering contaminated surfaces with sealants.

Other Preventive Measures

• Ensure your child eats well. A well-nourished body is less likely to absorb lead. Toddler diet should include adequate amounts of iron, calcium, vitamin C, zinc and protein.

• Keep your toddler's hands clean by teaching him to regularly wash his hands several times a day.

• Keep your home and its surroundings clean. Get rid of dust and paint chips using a disposable wet cloth. Choose vacuum cleaners with HEPA filters to effectively trap lead particulars and airborne allergens.

• Regularly inspect your child's playpen, crib, toys and bed for peeling paint.

• Identify then eliminate potential lead contaminants in your home.

• Test your tap water for lead and take necessary steps to filter out lead.

• If you suspect your child has been exposed to lead, consult your doctor and request to have your toddler's lead levels tested.

Traveling with Child in Tow

Traveling with toddlers brings a host of special demands for parents who are primarily responsible for their safety and well-being. Here are some handy tips to ensure a safer and stress-free trip for you and your child:

1. Plan ahead of time. List down the things that your child will need, from snacks to toys to keep them occupied. While it is the

responsibly of a carrier to carry the passengers safely to their destination, it is the responsibility of parents to take care and look after their children.

2. Make use of the child restraint system. If your child is under 40 pounds or 18.1 kilos, the US Federal Aviation Administration recommends the use of a restraint system.

3. Be prepared for possible emergencies. When traveling, every parent should be aware and well educated of the emergency procedures to ensure safety of the child. First, pay careful attention to the preflight briefing. Inquire flight attendants for emergency equipment such as life preservers for kids. If your child has a specific medical condition, make sure to inform the flight attendant.

4. Take essential items in carryon luggage. Be sure to have enough diapers, food, medicine and toys that will last through the entire trip. There is also the possibility of flight delays and lost luggage, so make

sure you carry your child's essentials, especially if they are on special medication or diet.

5. Keep your toddler under control all throughout the flight. It is the parent's responsibility and not the flight attendants to supervise your child. Do not allow your child to wander around unsupervised. They can easily reach for silverware items, cups of hot coffee and other hazards that will pose serious danger.

6. Sit your child far from the aisle. Children always enjoy roaming and exploring. Placing them near the aisle can expose them to injuries such as getting bumped by the service cart or another person passing down the aisle.

7. If in case the emergency oxygen masks are deployed, make sure to put on your own mask first. While some people feel it is somewhat cruel for parents to prioritize themselves, there is actually a practical reason behind this. By putting on the mask first, you avoid passing out before helping

your child and reduce the possibility of hypoxia—oxygen starvation of the brain.

8. Keep your child belted at all times. Turbulence can occur at any time without prior warning, so it is important to keep your child firmly belted at all times. If your child wants to get up and move around, make sure the seat belt sign is off.

9. Bring along safe toys. Avoid toys with sharp edges, unusually heavy or those than break easily. It is also a good idea to bring toys that your child does not often use to keep them preoccupied for a longer period of time.

10. Check with your doctor. Before the scheduled travel, have your doctor test and screen your child to ensure he is in good health If your child has special medications, make sure to have ample supply. It is also important to plan for unexpected aliments, such as for an allergic reaction, stomach bug or fever.

Chapter 8: Lesson On Consistency

What is consistency? The Oxford Dictionary defines it as conformity when applying something. In parenting, this means that you have to be, in a sense, predictable, especially when it comes to your reactions to your children's behavior. This is important because children are less likely to develop anxiety and more likely to have a clear understanding of the consequences of their actions if you are consistent. To illustrate this point, take note of the following scenario:

One day, a mother reprimanded her son when he failed to tidy up his room before going to bed. A few days later, the son did not clean up his mess again; however, this time, the mother took care of it because she is exhausted and giving her child a talking-to is just too stressful. The following weekend, the son left his room untidy once more, causing his mother to scold him and have him clean up the area.

The child in the example above is likely to become confused as to what to expect from his mom, as he probably won't be able to form an association between leaving his room in disarray and getting reprimanded. What he'll get from the encounters he had with his mother is the notion of unpredictability, which in turn can lead to anxiety. If the mother displays this kind of inconsistency with other things, the child won't be able to use consistency as a learning tool that will help him develop good behavior, thus affecting his social skills and how he deals with problems. He will also have to cope with the anxiety that comes with the parenting inconsistency of his mother, which may result in him becoming destructive and aggressive (the association between these two factors has been proven by studies).

How can you be consistent as a parent? Here are some tips:

Recognize the importance of consistency. Many parents fail to be consistent in dealing with their kids because they are not aware of how important this is to the development of their children. If you want to practice consistency, it is crucial that you are aware of what this can do for you and your kids. You should also know the consequences of being inconsistent.

Come up with a list of rules. You don't need to have a lengthy and detailed list; in fact, the simpler your list is, the easier it will be for you to implement the rules in it consistently. Once you're done creating the list, recite it to yourself every day until you commit it to memory. This practice may seem odd, but knowing the rules you set by heart will help you become more consistent when implementing them.

Be calm. One of the main reasons many parents are inconsistent is they find it hard to keep their patience in the face of arguments and other unpleasant behavior that their children might exhibit when told to do something. Losing your cool is understandable, especially if you have other responsibilities, but try to prevent it from happening as it might lead you to do things that will affect your consistency in parenting (like the mother cleaning up after her son in the example given above).

Don't be afraid to be flexible when necessary. Parenting consistency does not mean all your rules are absolute. For instance: even if your kids have a curfew, it's okay to let them sleep or come home at a later time on weekends or as a reward for good behavior. Just make sure, though, that you talk to them about it: let them know that you are aware of the change in the said rule and explain the deviation. This way, there won't be room for confusion and you're still consistent.

Make sure you're in sync with the other people who take care of your kids. Babysitters, nannies, daycare teachers, and even grandparents should be made aware of how you want your children to be treated. Of course, this does not mean you should go for total compliance. Leniency, for instance, can be exercised with the grandparents – especially if they don't see the kids often – but not to the point that they are contradicting what you teach your children. On a related note, make sure that you talk to your kids when you arrive from work or when they come home after staying at their grandparents' house or after school/daycare. Doing so will enable you to check if there's a consistency issue that needs to be addressed with any of the people mentioned earlier.

Chapter 9: How To Effectively Earn The 'Respect' Of Your Child

It all boils down to one thing when it comes to getting your children to listen to what you have to say to them: 'respect'. If you can get your kids to respect you, you will find that half your work is done. Let's take a look, then, at all the possible ways in which we can score brownie points where it comes to harnessing a greater level of respect from our children.

Respect them.

The very first thing you need to understand is that your children are every bit worthy of the kind of respect that you command from them and that if you do not respect them, the chances that they will respect you back are minimal. You have to make sure you respect them in order to gain the same level of respect back. It's really very easy – you will know intuitively when you are being disrespectful to them and those are the things you need to look out for in an attempt to curb them.

Respect your spouse.

One of the greatest things you could ever do is to respect your spouse in order to gain the same level of respect from your children. Of course, this does not mean that you respect them merely for your children (there is a reason that you are in a relationship with your spouse, right?). You have to ensure that your children actually witness the love and respect that you have for your spouse. See the huge difference it will make when it comes to them showing a greater sense of respect for you in the process.

Teach them the value of love.

The best way to get your children to love and respect you is to teach them the value of love. If you are merely trying to get them to obey you by being a disciplinarian while at the same time not teaching them the value of loving others, it will not have the same desired effect in making them understand exactly what the connection between love and discipline is. When you teach them the value of love they will understand the real 'need' for them to listen to what you are trying to tell them – that is the best possible way to discipline!

Don't let them walk all over you.

If you are in the habit of constantly caving in to your children's demands, you will find that it will become almost impossible for you to get them to listen to you at the time when they most need to. You have to make sure you do not let them walk all over you so when the time comes for them to really listen to you, they will most certainly comply with your wishes. There is no way that you are going to gain their respect if you constantly allow yourself to look disrespectful in their eyes.

Don't allow yourself to fall to their level.

Kids are famous for having temper tantrums, or losing their cool when things do not go their way. It would be the right thing to do to be as calm as you possibly can when talking to your children and explaining to them exactly why things should be the way you want them to be, in the most reasonable tone you can muster. That will show your maturity and enable them to respect you all the more!

Live with a sense of unparalleled integrity.

Your kids are going to be observing you all the time and they will pick up little things from you that will go a long way into molding their character; therefore when you go to a restaurant and tip the waiter generously for his exceptional service, you will find that this is something they pick up on. That will instill in them a strong sense of respect for others and in turn will ensure that the same level of respect extends towards you as well!

Talk about disrespectful situations in their aftermath.

When something has gone wrong when it comes to your child being disrespectful to you, there is really nothing you can do to change what has already happened. But you could sit down with your child afterwards in the process of showing them just how unpleasant the whole situation was and that it should not happen again. When your child gets in the process of reflecting on the things he or she might have said to you in a bout of anger, it gives them a chance to self-reflect and ensure that the same kind of behavior does not happen again.

Chapter 10: Challenge : New Responsibilities

One of the hardest adjustments for new parents is putting someone else first. It might be one parent is great at putting their child's needs first, while the other is still unable to make the adjustment. Whether both parents struggle, or just one, it is important to realize that the little life you have or are bringing into the world is wholly dependent on you. They need you to be there for their needs, particularly in the first eight to ten years.

Your child will need you to provide food, a place to sleep, and love constantly. As your baby starts to grow, crawl and walk there is a need to start teaching them words, how to talk, and developing their motor skills. By age two, your child's bladder is starting to develop to where your child can hold their needs to go to the bathroom and be trained to use the toilet.

The more independent you can make your children early on, the better. It does not mean you will not be needed, but studies have shown that a child who is potty trained when they show the inclination does better in their life. Holding a child back when they are ready for something will hinder your child later in life. They might start to cling to you more or ask for you to do things they can do.

You always have to put your child and their needs ahead of your own. It is also important to anticipate what your child requires before they need it. For example, anticipate the potty training, when they need new clothing, and the learning tools they will need.

Your Mindset Matters

You may think you have accepted your new responsibilities. You have nine months to accept that your life is going to change; however, sometimes it takes holding that baby in your arms or even several months after your child has arrived to realize just how much your life will change.

If you find you are having trouble accepting that your child will come first for the rest of your life, here are some steps to help you.

Remember why you wanted to have a child.

Consider that this little person depends on you to teach them love, and responsibility.

Set up times where you can have a "free night." Babysitters and family are great for spending a few hours with your children, so you can enjoy time alone.

Remember how you were raised. Were you raised as a secondary thought or the main person in your parent's life? How did you feel about that?

Parents who were raised as a secondary thought, as less important to a parent or both parents often feel they lack love.

Some can become all about themselves, with some narcissistic tendencies. If you have been through something like this, you know how it feels to be ignored or thought of second. Let your experience help you change your mindset. You can approach each day with a new goal to put your children first.

For those who were put first, remember how it felt? You probably felt well loved. Sometimes you might have been tired of the discipline and rules, but you learned it was all because your parents loved you and wanted you to be safe.

One of the best things a parent said once was, "I don't want to be like my mother. I was made to feel like I was a mistake or accident. I was told to do this and that, but never taught how to cook, do the laundry, and puberty was never explained to me, so I was scared when my body started to change. I want to be someone you can love, turn to, and know that you can depend on."

Those words resonated because this parent had already figured out that to be the best parent, she needed to put her children first—always.

If you have trouble adjusting to these new responsibilities, it is okay. Mistakes can be made. It will be the memories of the good times that far outweigh the mistakes made in life.

Never Forget to Take Time

There is nothing wrong with taking time for yourself. You had a life, hobbies, and activities you enjoyed. You may not be able to do everything you did before. For example, you may not be able to go out every night or spend money on certain things because you need it to raise your children. However, there is nothing wrong with hiring a babysitter or asking a close family member to sit with your children once a week.

Your children will grow up getting used to being away from you for short periods of time, which helps them become strong and independent. It also helps you keep a little enjoyment in your life, where you are first during those few hours.

Naturally, you are going to worry about your children. It will be tough at first to be away for a few hours, but you will be able to reset your emotions.

There is nothing wrong about wishing to put yourself first for a little while. Everyone needs a little time. It becomes a problem if you ignore your new responsibilities or always put yourself above your children's needs.

Chapter 11: Teen To Adulthood

Dealing with Difficulties

Just because something is difficult doesn't mean it isn't worth pursuing. For teenagers, beginning the process of separating from their parents is natural, but all too often it becomes a very painful experience for everyone concerned. Parents may rush to hold their teen back from becoming the inevitable adult they are destined to become, or the teenager may rush toward adulthood a little too fast and furious for their own good. The temperament of the teen and the parents often makes a huge difference in how smoothly the transition takes place.

Communication between the parent and the child has a tendency to slow or even completely shut down once a person enters their teen years. Nonetheless, parents need to not fear pushing through the sometimes-obnoxious body language of their teen to let their teenager know they are loved and a valued member of the family.

Body language is a defense mechanism that people of all ages use unconsciously. It's my opinion that too much weight is given to the meaning of body language. Hopefully, parents will over look their teen's glares, stares and rolling eyes and see the really scared person who lives inside that ever-changing body. Many psychologists purport that an emotionally impaired individual may put up such silent barriers to test your level of concern. Again, make sure your teen knows they are loved.

Life's Pressures

To say that only teenagers deal with peer pressure would be ignoring the social structure of world societies. Peer pressure is exerted on just about every human being on the face of the earth. Social norms are a basic part of any culture and that includes the local high school. Many adults look back on the peer pressure they experienced in their formative years and vow to never again be subject to such extreme or even repulsive activities. Yet, we see peer pressure everywhere from breast-feeding practices to protocol of the government's heads of state. Let's face it, peer pressure is a fact of life regardless of your age.

Nonetheless, as parents it's our duty to guide our children by teaching them our values, as well as to have self respect. It may be that you need to go the extra mile to support your child's ability to stand up for them self. Therefore, instilling in your child at a young age that they have a God given duty to be the individual they were created to be, and that they have an obligation to themselves and others make good choices will pay big dividends. Once they are faced with a difficult situation as teenagers they will be better equipped to resist participating in undesirable activities - which they would likely have preferred to opt out of anyway. Again, teaching children to make good choices should begin at the earliest age possible, and should include a discussion of the ramifications of making bad choices.

Chapter 12: Being The Best Step Parent Possible

Step parents have been criticized for a considerable length of time. The shrewd step parent is a typical prime example in TV, films and even tales. Actually, a cherishing step parent can be an intense power for good in a kid's life. Here is the way to conquer your step child's fears and maybe some of your own:

Building a strong step family

☐Survey the situation: While turning into another step parent, it is vital to take a seat with your partner and comprehensively talk about the changeover. Plan a period to talk through desires, duties, and obligations. Figure out whether, when and under what conditions it is adequate for you to discipline your step kid. Choose what your step kid ought to call you. Tell your partner you need to be the most ideal step parent to his/her youngster. Request your partner's understanding and backing as you explore this new part.

☐ Do tour research: Tap your life partner's comprehension of his/her youngster to figure out how to best identify with your step kid. What are your step kid's preferences and aversions? What communication and disciplinary styles work best with them? Requiring some serious energy to do a little research before all else can minimize future clash.

☐ Expect resistance: Step kids regularly oppose another step parent. Try not to expect the most exceedingly bad attitude that your step kid despises you. Regardless of the possibility that your step kid lets you know thus, do not trust it. Kids as often as possible test the limits of individuals they dread will at last reject or disillusion them.

If your life partner had various unsuccessful relationships before you, your step kid may address whether you will stick around. Tell your step kid that you cherish their mom/father, as well as are focused on him/her.

☐Exposing the reunion myth: A few kids may stick to the conviction that their natural parents will sometime get back together. The child may even think he/she can push you away, making a conjugation between his/her folks more probable. If so, your life partner may need to delicately remind your kids that specific dream is not going to happen for reasons completely unconnected to you.

☐Keep perspective: Try not to liken the awful states of mind portrayed above with being a terrible kid. These responses are typical for children adjusting to a blended family. The move to a changeover is no picnic for you; it is likewise troublesome for a youngster. The dominant part of changing will happen in the main year of marriage. Keep it together.

☐ Regard your spouse: Reliably demonstrating admiration to your partner is one of the snappiest approaches to win the appreciation of your step kid. Kids are actually defensive of their folks. By indicating thought to your partner, you end up being your step kid's partner, instead of his or her enemy. Some contention is unavoidable in a marriage. Simply recollect your step kid is viewing your treatment of your partner will direct their impression of you.

☐ Regard your spouse's ex: Regardless of the fact that your partner's ex does not appear to be deserving of appreciation, do not attempt to amplify it at any rate. Insulting your kid's other parent will expand pressures with your step kid and perhaps your partner too. At the point when communicating with your step kid's other parent, it is most likely best to give your partner a chance to set the guidelines.

☐ Tread lightly: In time, you ought to feel great attesting your power as a step parent. Particularly to start with, do whatever it takes not to put on a show of being bossy or controlling type. At first, your step kid will see you as a gatecrasher; it will set aside time for you to be seen as a naturalized subject of the family. This does not mean you ought to be a weakling or endure affront. Simply demonstrate some affability and attentiveness with respect to your new position in the family.

☐ Cash cannot buy you love: Fight the temptation to charm yourself to your step kid by purchasing regular or indulgent presents. Material merchandise would not win genuine love and may make improbable desires. The most ideal approach to win over your step kid is essentially to get to know one another, both as a family and one-on-one. The time you contribute becoming acquainted with your step kid says a lot. Recreational activities, family excursions, and amusements can break the ice and guide you both into a more profound relationship.

Updates for the biological parent: Your partner is strongly entering another family environment. Regardless of the fact that your partner has past child rearing knowledge, adjusting to the extraordinary society of your family can scare. Ensure your life partner feels like you have his or her back. In the event that your partner settles on a child rearing choice you cannot help contradicting, attempt to talk with him or her secretly about it. You will probably keep on being the essential slave driver and leader in connection to your youngsters, yet attempt to introduce an assembled front to the kids. If you transparently address your life partner's power, your youngsters will be more probable do as such as well.

Chapter 13: Behavior Management Tips & Tools

We've made a list of tips that will help you deal with issues that influence children's behavior.

1 - Fights can be difficult for a child. It's even worse if this conflict happened between the parents. Understand the importance of maintaining a harmonious home where feelings are accepted and discussed without judgment. Disregarding a situation that has been recognized by your child, can be harmful to their emotional development. If your child understands an argument or feels the tension in your home, explain that yes, his feelings are valid but that he is safe and loved.

2 - Letting your child make decisions and letting him dream about the future without fear will help him be a happier

and more confident child. Allow self-expression and applaud your child's desires. Reinforce and "I can do it!" attitude.

3 - Getting your child to know, appreciate, and respect other cultures is not only a cool thing to do, it can help them in the future. Understanding other ways of living will allow them to be more approachable and respectful, allowing for better relationships and success.

4 - Helping your child to feel loved and special, in addition to his siblings, can shape his identity and present him with a healthy sense of self-esteem in the present and future. Everyone needs to believe in themselves!

5 - Children lie and do not always understand the gravity of a lie. Understanding where they are in development is necessary here. Talking about what harm lies can cause is essential in developing their grasp on how all the world works.

6 - Teaching gratitude to your child creates a happier child and can be fun. People love good news, especially children. What's better than having something to be grateful for? Teach your children to be grateful for the small things such as the weather, their toys and clothes, the fun they have at the park, or even the hug they receive. There will always be something to be grateful for, and this way of thinking can change their world for the better.

7 - Humor is very important in the individual and social development of your child. Laughing is healthy. Being able to see the humor in situations can help build personality.

8 - Children are surrounded by issues that can cause anxiety and fear. Fear of the unknown is fear of most everything for young children, not to mention the size difference for a child in an adult world. Explore with your child and teach them to feel capable and safe.

9 - You may have heard about "The Terrible Two's". Be aware of what to expect from the tantrum phase. Most parents would agree that the terrible two's is referring to 2 and 3-year-olds. Remember to practice patience and understanding. Children at this stage are ready to communicate and get around on their own, and we need to convey to them that they are still learning. Make learning fun by giving them jobs as a helper with tasks you would normally do alone.

10 - Each of a child's actions has a meaning, but it is not always clear what it means. Pay close attention to the context of your child's behaviors, and you will understand what each behavior of your child means.

11 - This may seem like nothing to you, but for your child, it can mean a lot: Respect your child's growing emotional skills. Their knowledge of the world is rapidly expanding and can become overwhelming.

Never embarrass a child for feeling a certain way.

12 - It is normal for some children to feel uncomfortable in new situations. Giving them the rundown before you leave the house allows them to know what to expect and it can help with confidence.

Be Aware Of The Difficulties Of The Child

According to experts, persistent difficulties in performing tasks can indicate signs of hearing problems, vision or hyperactivity, and should be analyzed before raising the conclusion.

Certain behaviors may direct parents to find out if the child suffers from these disorders. It's important to pay attention to troubles your child may have and discuss them with your doctor regularly. All children develop differently, so don't jump to conclusions on your own.

Behavior Modification Techniques

The great number of learning studies carried out in the behavioral field (especially by B. F. Skinner on) allowed the delineation of an intervention methodology named Applied Behavior Analysis (ABA) and behavior modification. This technical-scientific approach aim to preventing, managing and solving children's behavioral problems. In this context, "behavior" refers to actions and abilities.

Below, I will explain to you the main evaluation strategies and educational intervention. Specifically, I will specifically focus on:

-procedures for proper observation of children's abilities and difficulties (behavioral assessment).

-I will focus on strategies to enhance positive behaviors and on strategies to decrease problematic behavior.

Skills And Behavior Assessment

-Consider the level of development of the child a precise evaluation of his abilities both in the cognitive and behavioral field.

To help you: download the free developmental checklist at the beginning of this book.

-Consider the strength and weak points of your child to organize suitable learning situations.

-A functional assessment aimed at understanding the motivations behind the behaviors. Check if there were any changes in the child's family life (for example, the birth of a brother), or if your child has slept enough and is in good health. Sometimes challenging behavior is the first sign to indicate that the child is not well.

Teaching Skills To Children: Strategies

As already stated, behavioral management involves educational work aimed at acquiring and consolidating various functional skills and competences. The main strategies used to acquire and consolidating skills and abilities in children are:

- Prompting and fading
- Modeling
- Shaping
- Chaining
- Reinforcement

Prompting And Fading

The technique is to provide the child with one or more stimuli in the form of instructions (Prompts), to achieve the desired skill. Prompts are usually obvious and are proposed at the exact moment the performance should occur. These can be divided into:

- Verbal suggestions
- Gestural indications
- Physical guidance

Depending on your child's level, they can be provided in the form of vocal verbal instructions (such as explaining, telling, etc.) and non-verbal (such as written, images, etc.). These prompts must necessarily be reduced or modified

(Fading) to allow the definitive integration of the ability in the behavioral repertoire of your child.

Modeling

Much of our learning is based on imitation. Much of what we have learned in our lives, we have learned from observing other people. In these cases, other people are the model for our behavior. The ability to imitate is, therefore, a requirement of great importance for human beings. The modeling technique consists in the proposal of learning experiences through the observation of the behavior of the subject that acts as a model.

The modeling technique is used when a parent intends to teach his child, through imitation, certain new behavior that he is unable to implement quickly through other modalities. This is a technique that allows reaching important goals at the level of behavior, but, above all at the relational level. It allows, in fact, to adapt the adult's expectations to achievable goals, avoiding making negative feelings on the child such as frustration, and establishing a virtuous spiral of reciprocal reinforcements: the adult reinforces the child for small improvements and such improvements reinforce the adult in return.

Shaping

In practice, with this technique, we will repeatedly reinforce those behaviors that, although far from the targeted behavior, progressively approach the goal.

B.F. Skinner describes shaping with the analogy, operant conditioning is compared to a ceramist who shapes a piece of clay. The ceramist's product will have a specific shape but we will not be able to find the precise moment in which this form will appear. Likewise, is a certain response from a child is not something that appears suddenly but the result of an ongoing process of formation.

Reinforcement must, therefore, be provided initially to behaviors that are relatively easy for the subject, and then reinforce those that are increasingly closer to the target behavior. To do this we need to break down the final objective into small sub-goals. In this way, we will reduce the expectation of the child. Gently pushing to his small improvements every time, until reaching the final goal.

Chaining

Chaining or step by step is a strategy used for teaching complex skills. When teaching complex skills such as personal autonomy like dressing, washing hands, brushing teeth, you need to split the tasks into small, separate steps to facilitate learning. When you use chaining, the first step is to prepare and complete a task analysis, identifying all the smallest teachable units of behavior that constitute a behavioral chain.

Task analysis to teach your child how to brush his or her teeth might look like this:

-Take the toothbrush

- Squeeze a small amount of toothpaste onto the toothbrush
- Wet the toothbrush under the tap
- Brush the teeth

There are two procedures for teaching a chain of behaviors: forward chaining and backward chaining. Using forward chaining, the behavior is taught in its natural order. Every single phase of the sequence is taught and reinforced once the entire sequence is completed correctly. Using backward chaining, all behaviors identified in the activity analysis are initially completed by the adult, except for the final behavior of the chain. Then it is the turn of the second last step and so on. An advantage of backward chaining is that the child has the feeling of having successfully completed a task before mastering the entire procedure. This gives to him confidence and motivates him to continue his efforts.

Reinforcement

Reinforcement is the most important and widely applied principle of behavioral analysis and regulates most of our daily activities. Reinforcement can be defined as a consequence that strengthens a given behavior with the chance that it happening again in the future.

Reinforcements can be of two different types: positive and negative. When it comes to behavior, positive and negative do not mean good or bad. They simply must be intended as algebraic signs that is the add and subtract. The positive reinforcement increases the probability that behavior is repeated thanks to the positive effect that this provides. For example, a child is learning to read, the mother is close to him and when the child reads correctly, she tells him: "good" (positive reinforcement); reading acquires a positive value for the child because for him it is a source of attention from the mother. Negative reinforcement also increases the probability that a behavior will be repeated because this removes a certain negative effect. For example, the child cries because she's hungry her mother rushes to feed her, in similar situations, when the child will be hungry, she will cry again to get her mother's attention. Negative reinforcement is not punishment. Punishment does not lead to the extinction of behavior but it will make it less likely to occur in the future.

In punishment, there is no learning. Certain behavior is inhibited, blocked (usually momentarily) without learning new behaviors. In reinforcement instead, both positive and negative, there is learning because in the case of positive reinforcement we learn a new behavior that has positive effects, in the case of negative reinforcement you learn a new behavior that is useful to stop something negative.

How to effectively use reinforcement when working to teach new behaviors?

- Reinforcements should be customized based on child preferences: observe the child's interests and motivation to determine which reinforcements are best.

- Reinforcement should be immediate: this means that the reinforcement should be delivered immediately after the desired behavior appears.

- Reinforcement must also be associated with behavior: in other words, the level of reinforcement must adapt to behavior.

- You associate tangible reinforcements to social reinforcements: sometimes it is important to combine praise with rewards.

- Continuous reinforcement and intermittent reinforcement: it is important to constantly decrease the number of reinforcements given over time.

Reinforcement is an important principle that determines an actual change in behavior. It is used in all ABA programs but it is also something that happens naturally in your everyday life. Think about your days and your life: you will realize that almost everything is driven by the principle of reinforcement and that all our behavior is encouraged or not by the response we get.

Below we will explain through simple examples four proven behaviors modification techniques.

Behavioral Intervention Techniques

Parent's behavioral intervention techniques are usually based on the consequences of a child's behavior. Those interventions attempt to change behavior through the application of positive or negative consequences. Positive and negative consequences increase or decrease the frequency, intensity and duration of a given behavior, they are used as rewards or sanctions.

When applied correctly, positive consequences can be very effective in modifying children's behavior. Experience suggests that whenever positive consequences are immediate, regular and modified in order to avoid a certain habit, children can reach good results. The first step that parents have to do to intervene with positive consequences, is to observe the child's actions in order to determine which consequences can be truly reinforcing for the child, that is, which prizes, situations or actions are effective to strengthen the desired behavior.

The use of negative consequences for the child can be carried out through some techniques including planned ignoring, the cost of answer and time-out. Since the negative consequences are effective regulators of human behavior, these must be applied adequately and safely in a controlled environment.

Time-Out

The time-out can be used in two ways. One of these is the typical reaction to unwanted behaviors: "go to your room for five minutes" or "sit for five minutes in punishment." This type of time-out will be seen by the child as a negative conclusion or punishment. Probably, the most effective approach is to think at time-out as a pause to the child's poor behavior and not as a punishment, a short period of time that allows the child and the parent to have a few minutes to distance themselves from negative behaviors, in order to process them and calm down.

What happens after the time-out is very important! Some believe that, after a time-out and before anything else, the child has to come back and apologize. Others instead conceive time-out as time spent moving away from negative behavior and then being able to rejoin the family without the embarrassment of having to apologize publicly. This second modality is preferable because it allows the child to reconnect more naturally to the activity interrupted and, on the other hand, avoids the emotional problems linked to having to apologize.

Cost Of Response

This technique is used to remove something pleasant from the child. In other words, fines or penalties will be applied when negative behavior occurs. We use the cost of response to avoid providing the child with feedback to inappropriate behavior in conjunction with positive rewards for appropriate ones. For example, if the child doesn't observe some previously established rules, this procedure involves the loss of a previously earned token or the failure to earn one in the future: "If you don't want to take the coat off the ground, I'll do it but you'll lose a token ".

Token Economy

The establishment of a Token system at home is quite simple. The basic idea is that a child earns tokens every time he achieves an established goal. If the child fails to reach the goal there are no negative consequences; tokens are in fact assigned only to the achievement of the goal or positive behavior. Once a token is earned, this can never be taken away. This allows the child to form a strong link with positive choices. In some cases, as previously mentioned, it is also possible to earn extra credits in order to further incentivize the child's motivation toward positive behaviors. For example, if the child helps to lay the table, as agreed, he earns a token; in addition, if he also offers himself to help to clear up, he could earn additional credit.

To create an effective Token Economy it is necessary to think carefully about the way the table is presented. This needs to contain the description of goals to achieve and relative rewards, also evaluate where to place it in order to make it visible.

Positive Communication

The way we choose to communicate is absolutely important. Rather than say "don't do this or that" we try to communicate our intent using descriptive and positive sentences. "Don't swear" could be expressed as "we use polite language" or "we speak to people respectfully"; "Don't hit" the same way, it could become "we use our hands gently". Try to contain comments and negative reactions. Our interventions, including Token Economy, will be less likely to succeed if we use a punitive tone of voice or aggressive body language. The child may change some of his behaviors for fear of being punished, but this will not help him to grow. Moreover, when the fear is no longer present, the child's behavior will again tend to worsen.

If the child behaves as we expected, reward him by identifying a precise moment and a place. For example, before going to the mall we could say: "If you sit calm and safe while driving, you will receive a reward of two tokens", or "if you sit politely at dinner, at the end of the meal you will get a cake". With these sentences, we have made an accurate and positive description. Always remember to describe the behavior you want.

Chapter 14: Dealing With Toddler Tantrums

Now with all the theories and techniques laid before you from the previous chapters, now is the time to put all of them in practice. How do you stay composed as your toddler starts to scream and cry louder and louder? How do you deal with a child who refuses to hear your commands? And what about those regular tantrums?

Tantrums are a toddler's trademark. They start at around their first year until such time that they are able to find ways to get what they want when they want it. While children are born different, some you can easily control, there are others with a short fuse. Disciplining them would mean expecting that there will be a mess all around.

In a toddler's eyes, a tantrum can be brought about by many different stimuli. This can be from inner frustrations or him being impatient of himself and others. To treat tantrums, it would rely greatly on the age your toddler is in. From ages 1 to 2 1/2 years, your toddler's behavior can be soothed with gentleness and a good dose of understanding. At the age of 3, a child uses a tantrum to resist his parents' orders. This is where you should be consistent and firm enough in your rules. Let this point be clear to him that there is no way he can get things his way and throwing a tantrum is not just worth the effort.

Tantrums – The Major Battle

Every day, you are confronted with many different kinds of tantrums. On center stage is a child who is being prevented from doing something that will either endanger him or the things around him. Notice that first, he takes a good look at his surroundings in preparation for one spectacular show. Next, he takes a look at his audience and their reactions. And then finally, in just a flash, he does it and the performance of his lifetime is on.

Tackling tantrums may not be an easy one, but they can be dealt with. Take a look at the following examples and see how you can handle tantrums of different kinds:

There are ideal methods for handling tantrums based on the reason for the tantrum in the first place

This is where you need to assess the situation and your surroundings to decide why is the tantrum happening in the first place. Once you know the reason for the tantrum you can take the appropriate response. Here are the main three reasons tantrums happen and the guidelines for dealing with each one:

The child wants your attention. If the Child is throwing a tantrum for your attention, pay them no attention whatsoever. If you can, leave the room, you will thus be removing their audience and showing them it is not an effective way to get what they want. You'll find that this might cause them to up their antics in a desperate case to win your attention back. However, they will not continue this too long once they realize it isn't working. it might take a couple of goes but stick to it. If you give in once they'll see a chink in your armor so you have to stick to your guns on it.

If the tantrum is because of your child's inability to communicate what they want or if it's because of their inability to do something that's causing them to be frustrated then: Firmly explain that their behavior is not ok and then to figure out a way to encourage them and help them. Teach them that if they are patient and they don't give up, they can succeed. This will also help them to develop this quality that will carry through with them for the rest of their life.

If a child is being deliberately destructive or is in danger of harming others; a time out is in order. Take your child and place them in their room or in a safe space alone. Sometimes children struggle to calm down on their own, however. Activities such as singing a song or an activity might help.

On tidying up toys

While some children seem to be born organized and tidy, the majority are quite messy, and they love being like that. The former can be easily trained, while the latter would be a bit challenging. To make things easier for parents like you, you can try the following tips:

Try restricting the number of toys your toddler has.

Allot a big box for toys and make it a habit to let your child clear up his toys and put them in the box after playing. Tidy up with your child and have it be a fun time for both of you.

Make tidy not just a habit but also a form of play. The moment you say the word "Tidy", have your toddler pick whatever toy lying on the floor and put it inside the box. Make this fun and exciting for your little one.

Change Their Emotions Not Their Mind

Toddlers have not yet developed the ability to use logic and reason. There is no point trying to win on this front. Instead, try changing the circumstances completely. The scenarios that lead to a child getting angry or throwing tantrums can often be changed. When you change the way the child perceives an event, the event itself changes. Try to flip the script on the child, if they hate meal times, try to think of a way you could add something in, that's enjoyable for both of you. Maybe you devote some attention to them. You could have a race to see who could tidy up the fastest.

When you start getting angry, the child cannot always understand why. Often toddlers can be like quicksand; the more you struggle, the quicker you sink. You can try shouting and using force all you want.

Instead, sometimes it's best to go the opposite way and be almost devoid of emotion on the topic at hand. If they get next to zero emotional response from you, it is not satisfying for them. You can reward them when they do good, however when they do bad, be firm and tell them, but try to take emotion out of it. Your child's emotions are their main driving force if you learn to guide their emotional state you will learn to guide them.

Build a rapport with the child

A rapport is building a relationship with the child where it's clear you understand each other's feelings and concerns. If the child is upset try, understand where they are coming from. If the child can sense you have built a rapport with them, they are more likely to feel the concerns understood and less likely to act out. It is how you are making them feel that matters, not trying to outsmart them with logic, they don't speak that language yet. This helps you better understand your child. If your toddler refuses to share their toy, trying going down to their level(this helps in building rapport) and asking them about it. Sometimes a child just needs to experience owning something before they are ready to give it away. You want to instill the belief that this is ok and that it would be great if they did share, it would make you really happy but ultimately they have a choice. This will teach your child to do things like sharing because they want to and not because they have to.

How to build a rapport with a child

To try and build a rapport with the child: firstly as stated before, get down to their level and try to feel what they're feeling and empathize with them. An example in the adult world of this is: If two people meet and one of them starts telling them of something bad that happened them, it would be strange if the second person didn't meet their emotional state. Imagine you were telling them something that really hurt you, and they stood there smiling, you wouldn't feel very understood. So try putting yourself in your child's shoes and feeling what they're feeling when you are listening to them.

Use positive instead of negative language

It is a human quality to want to do something when we are told we can't. Instead of asking your child to stop messing around, ask them could they stand still. Instead of saying don't touch that, ask them can they keep their hands by their side. When we tell them they can't do something, it creates this irresistible urge a lot of the time to do the very thing we're telling them not to. The same psychological drivers that exist in us as adults exists in children.

Chapter 15: Toddlers

When your baby becomes a toddler, there are new challenges that you will have to face. At this point in their lives, your child will start becoming curious about their world, as well as with the things they encounter and the people they mingle with both at home and when outdoors. They will begin to learn new things, including some significant skills that they will use for the rest of their lives such as walking. In connection to this, once your baby becomes a toddler, you will also need to be there to teach her things regarding personal hygiene and communication. It is an exhausting yet very rewarding part of both the parent's and the baby's life.

If you are the type of parent who is completely devoted to taking care of her baby, then you will have an almost unending supply of patience and perseverance which are needed in raising your toddler. However, if you are like most parents who still need to go to work in order to pay the bills, or do other chores such as cook for other members of the family after getting off from work, then patience with your toddler might be something that you do not have a generous supply of. When your baby turns to a toddler, everything that you do with them – from feeding to sleeping – becomes a big challenge. The rule for parents on most occasions is to prevent engagement with their child.

Crucial to Parenting...

In order to make less trouble when you take care of your toddler, make sure that you let them try things out for themselves. Your job is to help them when needed, but not to control whatever it is that they are doing. Either you can turn routine tasks into fun games, or you can ask for your toddler's help. For instance, when it is time for your toddler to dress up, you can ask him to find the specific shirt she is to wear in her drawer. When her time begins to run out, give your toddler nicely-worded warnings informing her that if she does not find it, you are going to have to look for it instead. This will help them realize that they can take charge of some of the things that they need to do. On the other hand, you can also play peekaboo with them while they dress.

Potty-Training

Another thing that your toddler needs to learn is to use the toilet. Obviously, every parent looks forward to the day when they no longer need to spend so much money on diapers and they no longer have to clean up their baby's dirty bottom. However, if your child is not ready to be potty trained, you really would not be able to train her. So, when exactly is the right time to train your child to use the toilet by herself?

By the time that your child turns a year old, they will gain the awareness of the fact that the puddle on the floor directly underneath them or the wet feeling that comes from their diapers comes from them. However, they might not have the proper control over their bowel movements or their bladder, and so they might simply be limited to just being aware of what is happening versus actually being able to do something about it. Within the course of a few months, you would be able to tell if your child begins to get that feeling, and oftentimes when they say that they have to go, they literally mean that they are going right now. There would be no time for your child to rush to the toilet bowl or even lower her pants.

However, when your child reaches the age of two and a half, she would have the needed body control as well as the communication skill that is needed in order to tell you when she has to go to the bathroom. The best advice in teaching your child to do their elimination in the toilet seat is to take it slow. There will be times when your child will fail to do it perfectly, and if they do not, never show sign of frustration, and never resort to punishing, shaming, or blaming your child for their mistakes. You have to encourage your child to do it better next time. Even if they miss, tell them that they did a good job.

Chapter 16: Raising A Healthy Child

They say that you are what you eat. That is true. But raising a healthy child is more than just making him eat healthy foods and consume the right vitamins. In this chapter, you will find many ways to help your child develop healthy habits.

Encourage him to play active games. An hour of physical activity per day may sound like a burden but one hour is too short if you're having fun. Keeping your child physically active will help him develop his motor skills. These days, most children are fond of video games or online games. These activities will only affect your child in a negative way such as making him too lazy to walk or play outside. If you want to help your child become more active, don't simply leave him by himself. Play with him.

Here are some active things that you can enjoy with your child:

Blow bubbles and let your child chase them.

Play ball games such as soccer or basketball.

Go for short walks together at the park.

Plan family outings that involve active activities. For example, go swimming or mountain climbing. Allow him to see the wonders and beauty of nature.

Pay attention at the amount of time your child spends in front of the screen. TV and computer can keep your child inside the room for hours. Limit his access to TV and computer. Plan exciting activities to replace web surfing or TV watching.

Provide healthy meals at home. If you can, avoid junk foods and sodas. Healthy food doesn't magically appear on your dining table. You need to prepare them so as a parent, you have the responsibility to serve your family with healthy meals.

Find an exciting way to plan healthy meals with your child. Allow him to get involved in the process of preparation. You may want to plant a garden and let your child help you cultivate the plants. Bring your child with you when picking fruits for snacks.

The most important thing here is to set a good example to your child. You can't force your child in doing something you don't even practice. He needs to see you eating healthy meals and living a healthy lifestyle in order for him to understand the significance of healthy living.

Chapter 17: Refusal To Eat And Playing With Food

The first thing that you need to know when it comes to your toddler refusing to eat is that a child is not going to starve themselves to death. The child is going to eat enough food and is not going to go hungry, so you do not have to try and force your child to eat.

A toddler may decide that they are only going to eat one or two specific foods for two or three weeks at a time, then all of a sudden, they will want nothing to do with those foods and move on to something else.

While we all want to provide our children with perfect well-balanced meals, most of the time, a toddler is not going to be interested in these types of meals. You should not expect your toddler to enjoy the same food as you, and you should not stress out when the only thing the toddler will eat is bananas or some other food for weeks at a time.

The first thing that you can do to encourage your toddler to eat what is prepared for them is to make sure that there is structure at meal time. I highly suggest that you avoid the drive-thru and take out or delivery because that is setting your child up for failure when you do sit down at the dinner table to a prepared meal.

Instead, make sure that you are planning your meals ahead of time, ensuring that you are not planning on making a difficult dinner on a night when you are very busy. There are many different ways to ensure that your family is getting a home cooked meal each night and not relying on the local drive-thru when it comes to meal time. You can use crock pot meals, freezer meals or simply learn how to plan ahead.

It is also important that dinner time is about the same time every single night so that your toddler becomes accustomed to eating dinner at that time each day. This will ensure that the child is hungry when meals are placed in front of him or her.

One of the main reasons that children refuse food at meal time is because they are not being given the food at the same time each day. Their bodies cannot get used to eating at different times of the day, and they may not actually be hungry until later in the evening.

It is important that the child knows that everyone will be sitting at the dinner table and eating together. This seems to have fallen by the wayside in recent years, so many families are taking their food and going their separate ways at meal time instead of spending the few minutes together talking about their day.

It is also important that you teach the child that they need to try each of the foods on their plate. It takes up to 30 times for a child to taste a type of food before they begin to enjoy it so do not get discouraged if you feel that your child is rejecting the food that you prepare.

On that note, you need to make sure that you are preparing food that a toddler will actually eat. So often, I see parents making the mistake of preparing huge fancy meals for dinner expecting that their toddler is going to enjoy them when all the child really wants is a few pieces of chicken and some green beans.

Making sure that the toddler is actually able to feed themselves is also important. You do not want to give the child food that is too complicated for them to get into their mouth. Remember, the child is learning about his or her own independence way from you, he or she is going to want to feed themselves and if they cannot, chances are you are going to have a tantrum on your hands.

Let the child have a few choices when it comes to meal time. Ask the child if they want carrots or green beans, letting the child feel a sense of independence. This will increase the chances of the toddler actually eating the food that you place in front of him or her.

Do not threaten the child when it comes to meal time by telling the child that they will not get story time or some other activity that they are looking forward to if they do not eat their food. They genuinely may not be hungry or they may simply not like the taste of the food. As I said before, there is no reason to try and force the child to eat.

Along those same lines, you should not try to bribe the child into eating by offering some type of sweet reward, such as a cookie if the child eats a certain food. If you want to make sure that your child learns how to eat healthy as they grow, you need to make sure that mealtimes are a positive experience and NEVER offer sweet treats as a reward.

Do not feel that you have to stop serving a certain food simply because the child spit it out the first time they tried it. Chances are if you serve the food a few more times, the child is going to begin eating it regularly. However, you should prepare yourself for a few rejections before the child accepts it into his or her diet.

Remember that when a child drinks milk or juice with a meal, they are going to get fuller simply because they are drinking. It is recommended that you only serve water with your meal and only serve a small amount. If someone is actually thirsty after they have finished their meal, they can then have more water, but make sure that your toddler is not filling up on liquids instead of filling up on actual food.

It is also vital that you ensure that your child is not filling up on junk food before meal time. Junk food, sweet treats, and processed foods are not going to provide your child with any nutrients that he or she needs to grow. The reason that these foods are called junk food is because that is what they are, junk. If your child is hungry between meals, offer a healthy snack. This will ensure that even if the child is not hungry at meal time, he or she is still getting the vitamins and nutrients that they need.

Many parents spend a lot of money on vitamin supplements for their children, but the truth is, unless your doctor has specifically requested that you put your child on a vitamin, they are not needed. There was a time when the supplements were needed to ensure that children were getting the necessary nutrients, but it is simply not a necessity any longer. We have access to all the healthy foods that we need, and as long as you, the parent, are ensuring that you are providing your child with healthy meals, you do not need to worry about extra vitamins or supplements.

Now we get to why toddlers want to play with their food, throw food, or try and start food fights with other members of the family. The short of it, it's fun. There really is more to it than that, but toddlers like to have fun and what could be more fun than smearing, throwing and playing with something as messy as food?

There is some good news when it comes to your toddler playing with his or her food, and that is that it is normal. Studies have actually shown that toddlers who play with their food have a higher IQ than those who do not. So while it may drive you crazy, and you may hate cleaning up the mess, you can celebrate a little bit knowing that you are raising a very smart little person.

Playing with food is part of learning, it is something that toddlers do so that they can learn about the texture of the food that they are eating, and it helps them to identify these foods later. Playing with food is also fun, and since we all know that toddlers are little clowns, they love to be laughed at. If there is an audience, for example, siblings laughing at the toddler as they toss food about, the toddler is going to be encouraged to continue to do so.

While it is important to let the toddler play with their food sometimes, there should also be some rules in place, for example, when you are out eating, you do not want the people at the next table to be hit with food. Here are some of the ways to discourage a toddler from playing with their food.

Instead of placing a plate of food in front of the toddler, place one bite at a time on the toddler's tray and once that has been eaten provide another bit of food. You can use small bits of fruit, vegetables, or meat and let the toddler have a single piece at a time. Providing the child with a large portion of food is going to encourage messing, and when you are out at a restaurant or a friend's house, you want to discourage it as much as possible.

If you find that the toddler is only messing and throwing food because they have an 'audience' laughing at them, make it clear to older siblings that if they are going to encourage the toddler to make a mess, they are going to be responsible for helping to clean up the mess. After the siblings help clean up mashed up peas and sticky fruit from the floor and walls, they will not be so happy when the toddler begins throwing food and will not encourage him or her by laughing.

Teach the child that it is okay to play with their food since it is normal, but it must be kept under control. We all expect to have to clean the high chair when the toddler is done eating, but we do not want to spend hours scrubbing the walls and the floor. Therefore, allow the child to play with the food on the high chair tray, but as soon as the food leaves the tray, is thrown across the room or hits the floor, put an end to mealtime. Take the toddler out of the high chair, clean him or her up and end mealtime for the toddler. This will teach the toddler that when food leaves his or her tray, mealtime and fun time is done.

Distract the child if all else fails. Placing something small in the child's hands such as two plastic spoons or small toys while you feed the child is a great way to keep the child preoccupied while you make sure that your child is getting the food that he or she needs and that no mess is being made.

While it is tempting to always control the situation and to make sure that there is never a mess made when your child is eating, it is important to allow your child some freedom when it comes to playing with food. You have to allow your child to explore food, understand the textures and build a healthy relationship with it if you want them to be healthy as they grow.

Chapter 18: Motivate And Praise

A golden key factor towards boosting up the self-confidence and esteem of your child, and towards formulating a strong independent and ambitious individual is undeniably meeting your child's well-done activities and actions with praise and motivation towards performing the same actions and even better in the forthcoming times. Children actually expect to receive motivation and praise from you even for the simplest of actions done by them, even if you perceive these actions as too "superficial" or too "simple" to be praised for. We assure you, it makes a huge difference to your little one and really, really matters. In this context, you should always bear in mind the difference between the perspective of your child (which is developing and under construction) and yours (which is supposed to be at an advanced level). Accordingly, what you perceive as simple, superficial or trivial can actually be of utmost importance to your child.

If you do not give words of encouragement and support to your child for a simple achievement, huge disappointment is expected to overwhelm them (also here, bear in mind how sensitive a child can be!). This disappointment with the negative energy and vibes that accompany it, can significantly refrain the child and demotivate them from going any further in their endeavours. We have spoken previously about the importance of you becoming your child's first best friends. The same principle is applied here – you are supposed and expected to be the first ones to supplement your child with motivation and encouragement all the way before receiving it from the exterior. You must not be the reason of your child growing up to seek approval and encouragement granted to them by people other than you to compensate for what you had deprived them of.

Be aware here, we are not insinuating that your child should not get motivation from others, rather stating that your child should not seek it from others as a compensation. In a normal healthy case, in which your child is receiving praise and motivation from you in the first place, any similar reactions from the exterior would be certainly favourable and pleasant to receive, but this time would be secondary and not compensatory for your ungenerousness! Once again, and similarly to what we have explained above, you must be the number one source of motivation and support to your little one, so that your child could in the long run lean on you for support, being comfortable and secure, when the surrounding medium for any possible reason continues to demotivate, devastate and frustrate them.

Chapter 19: Vehicle Ownership

Receiving that dreaded call in the middle of the night from your teenager that they are in the middle of nowhere and are having car trouble is the worst. You have to get up, turn on your brain, and try to find out where they are to go and help if you can't do so over the phone. It is really not ideal.

Once your child moves out of home you might expect these calls to stop, or at least be directed to someone else. Don't be fooled though, they will still come your way. I have had several interrupted night's sleep, calls during work, and calls while I am out at dinner to prove that to myself.

From my experiences I now have an idea of the most common things that a teenager/adult will call their parents about with regard to their cars. This is great for you as we can prepare your child with a lot of the tools that they will need to get themselves out of trouble instead of you having to drop everything to offer assistance.

Lesson #16 purchasing and maintaining a vehicle

Unless your teen has an active interest in cars you no doubt will have had a lot of input into the vehicle that they drive and the maintenance that it has received to this point. My husband went with our children to look at, test, and negotiate the purchase of both of their first cars. He then did all of the oil changes and any minor repairs for them and made sure that the cars were registered and road legal. That is a pretty handy parent to have in my opinion.

But as children do, they come to expect that we will drop everything to assist them if anything goes wrong. If we did it in the past then surely we would be happy to do the same for the foreseeable future. This can result in your teens treating your home as a mechanics workshop. "Hey I am just going to drop the car and take yours for a few days until mine is fixed. Ok?" - Not ok.

Lessons in purchasing and maintenance

When you find a car that you want to purchase have a mechanic come out and test it for you. My daughter in NZ has done this with her last 2 cars and it cost her $85 each time. This might seem expensive to your teenager who probably does not have much money, but if the engine fails in a major way after a month or two it will cost them a whole lot more than the mechanical check.

Change the oil every 10,000 kilometers. If you do not it can lead to all sorts of internal engine problems that they do not need. Your teen does not have to learn to change the oil themselves, but if they do have the tools and the skills it can save a lot of money over a lifetime.

Get a full service once a year. This ensures that a qualified mechanic checks over all of the vitals of the car and can pick up on anything that is failing. It can be an expensive exercise, but if anything major is found to be failing in their car it could also save your child from having an accident.

It also pays to check your oil levels every couple of weeks to make sure that if their car is leaking oil that you are not driving around with a dry engine. This wears down the engine incredibly fast without oil to lubricate the moving parts and can lead to major, expensive problems.

Make sure to replace bald tires. In some countries the minimum tread requirement on tires needs to be 4mm or more. 4mm is almost nothing, and is actually quite dangerous to drive on. Your teen will not have as much traction in wet or slippery conditions, and if they get a puncture while driving they could have a major accident.

Key Takeaways

By letting your teen know that you expect them to take responsibility for their vehicles once they leave home you can save yourself a lot of extra work. It is important that you outline these expected maintenance points for them to adhere to as it ensures their safety on the road.

Knowing that your teen is driving a car that has been checked and maintained by a certified mechanic will give you added piece of mind when they are going on road trips and excursions.

Lesson #17 Tools to keep in the car

There are certain tools that are essential to keep in every car. Without them very simple problems to solve such as a flat battery, or a flat tire become major issues.

If your teen is out at a party and gets a flat battery and no one has jumper leads, they will call you. If they get a flat tire and cannot change it, they will call you. If they are stuck in the dark and don't know what is wrong with the car, they will call you. By making sure that they have the following items in the car you can either avoid these calls completely, or be able to step them through the fix over the phone.

Recommended tools for every car

Jumper leads

Tire iron - that fits the wheel nuts on that specific car

Car jack

Spare tire

Multi head screw driver

Flashlight

When my children were old enough to get their first cars I put together a 'car package' for each of them as a Christmas present. You might not want to go about this in the same way but make sure that your teen has these items in their car before leaving home or going on a long road trip.

Key Takeaways

Knowing that you're teen has the tools to fix the situation on hand then you do not need to drop what you are doing and rush to their aid. You can walk them through the fix over the phone. By giving your teen the tools that they need to overcome such problems you are empowering them to solve their problems on their own. This is essential to them becoming an adult and feeling comfortable living away from home.

Lesson #18 Changing a tire

Before I was ever allowed to get behind the wheel of a car I had to learn how to change a tire. The same was true for my two kids. The reason for it is that a flat tire is one of the most common things to fail on a vehicle and attempting to change a tire without knowing what to do can be extremely dangerous. So if your teen does not already know how to change a tire on their car lets teach them before they leave home.

How to change a tire

Step 1: Take out the jack, tire iron, and spare tire from the car.

Step 2: Loosen the wheel nuts on the flat tire while the car is on the ground. This is important as doing it while the car is up on a jack and jolt the car and cause the jack to roll and the car to fall on top of the person changing the tire - in this case your child.

Step 3: Put the jack down next to the wheel cavity that you are changing. This should be in the center of the car under the front or rear door and not under the bonnet or the trunk of the car.

Step 4: Jack the car up so that the flat tire is no longer touching the ground.

Step 5: Remove the wheel nuts and the flat tire.

Step 6: Put on the spare tire and screw in the wheel nuts until they are snug but not fully tightened.

Step 7: Lower the car down until the spare tire is touching the ground, but not so far that the suspension is taking the weight.

Step 8: Use the tire iron to tighten the wheel nuts as much as possible.

Step 9: Lower the car off of the jack and put tools back in the car.

Key Takeaways:

Before they leave home your children should know how to properly change a tire on their car. If they do not then they will be putting themselves at risk by driving alone should they get a flat as they will either be stranded or in danger of attempting to change it and getting it wrong. You do not have to be an expert yourself, but make sure that you teach this lesson to your teen before they leave home.

Chapter 20: Effective Communication: How To Talk To And Listen To Your Toddler.

Communication with your child represents an open door. The child will often initiate a conversation (sometimes it can be an open invitation for help), but the question is whether you will recognize this call for help, hear it, and answer it with an adequate response. If you invest in communicating with your child, this communication becomes the foundation on which you will build a lasting relationship.

Some of the basic laws of good communication with your child are:

Consider their age. You can already begin to explain the "great" secrets of life to your three-year-old child. It is surprising, but your toddler can understand how children are born, whether there is a God, what happens when someone dies, and similar things. Still, when you are talking to a child, the principle is always the same: tell the truth using words the child is already familiar with.

Communication is a two-way street when you share your everyday experiences with a child rather than expecting them just to talk to you. If you get a detailed answer to the question of how your toddler spent the day, the child deserves to receive a detailed answer to his question as well.

Share your personal opinions. You don't have to always keep things in confidence just because of the different level of a child's thinking. On the contrary, it is your duty to always state your opinion, that is, what you believe to be right, but in a manner that does not hurt your child, does not diminish him or her, or underestimate him. Just talk.

Always show your child enough patience and time to talk. If your toddler grows up with the conviction that he still has contacts with his parents - he will feel safer and happier. Try setting priorities. If your toddler wants to talk to you while you are doing some housework, let your child do so.

Communication is learned. Occasional quarrels, conflicts, and misunderstandings are common and typical occurrences in communication. But never give up.

Speech is given to us, but conversation is learned. We all can hear, but to understand, we have to put effort, time, and love into learning to listen.

How to control child's aggression

From time to time, your child gets bruises and scratches not only from taking a fall but also from playing games with their friends. Children have always played "mother and daughter" and "catch." It might seem like you could just say to your child: "Give the doll to Katie, you're a good girl!" But even if your child does it, you may not know what feelings are at work inside her: maybe she will get the impression that it's not so good to be good.

If you see or suspect how difficult it is for a two-year-old child to part with their favorite toy for the sake of good manners, it is better not to push the child and not to bring on hysterics.

When your toddler becomes a little older and has more experience in communicating, it will be easier for him or her to focus in similar situations, and as far as possible – to try to predict them.

Often, parents are afraid of another type of situation, in which their child might be aggressive, taking a toy from another child. Almost all kids struggle if they are somewhat dissatisfied and behave badly if they are tired. Sometimes the aggressiveness of the child takes the form of your toddler biting other children. This is basically the same situation.

As long as a quarrel doesn't lead to outright aggression on the part of one or more of the children, parents should not interfere. If there is a need to intervene, do not try to find the culprit: for one of the children, your decision will still be unfair.

It is better to separate the fighters and divert their attention to other activities. If you see that one of the children is constantly antagonizing your child, look for another circle of friendship, at least for some time, where the relationship between children will be somewhat different. The same can be done if your child is too aggressive with other children.

If you observe a situation in which your two-year-old child is beating other children, don't spank them or physically discipline them in any way, and, of course, do not ask another child to do it.

Perhaps your toddler is too small to respect other children. This respect needs to be learned gradually. Take the child aside and at the same time explain that the other child is hurt and that your child needs to apologize to him or her. If there is an opportunity, let your bully play with older children- in that type of environment, it will be harder for them to try to prove their strength. Note: the older the child, the more selective your toddler will be regarding demonstrations of his own aggressiveness towards other people. Most likely, children are aware of when they can get away with it and when they cannot.

In any case, children should be taught systematically to share toys.

If your child reveals an aggressiveness that frightens you, you have to think: perhaps its origins lie in the relationships that have developed in your family. Don't forget that you are an example to your child. And yet, the skills of exhibiting a good attitude towards each other are better instilled when the child is in good humor.

Outpouring of feelings

There is no doubt that you have an endless supply of love for your toddler.

Teach your toddler to be concerned about everyone around them. Let them help you during cooking: put the dishes on the table with you, put out bread and fruit. And you should accompany their actions with encouraging words. Of course, it will take more time to do the work than if the child wasn't "disturbing you," but you have learned that feeding a child is not all there is to raising him or her. Remember this.

You might put a doll or a toy animal down to sleep, gently stroking them "before bed," saying that they've been good and obedient. Ask your toddler to show how he or she loves the doll or toy animal.

Show your toddler how to take care of flowers, paying attention to the fact that they have beautiful small and delicate leaves and flowers.

When you go for a walk, take food for birds or squirrels in the park, feed them together, and praise the toddler for it.

If the child is sad or over-excited, then perhaps he won't do what you ask of him (maybe he will break a leaf or throw a doll on the floor or won't want to feed the animals).

This temporary act of aggression does not indicate bad character traits at all.

A sense of parental love and tenderness gives a child the opportunity to feel good and desired and gives him or her confidence in life.

What is good and what is bad ...

While a baby is small, the main prohibitions given by the parents are related to the concern for his or her safety. But always, when forbidding something and saying the word "No," do not forget to explain why and to tell the child how to do what he needs to do. In addition, parents should know that praise is much more instructive than prohibiting things.

As often as possible, show approval for the good things your toddler does, especially those that were hard for them. Do not simply give them prohibitions. According to psychologists, verbal prohibition is not meaningful for a child up to five years old.

The best solution to any problem is its joint discussion. If possible, examine the forbidden object that interests the baby together. Remembering the age of the child, try to find an explanation to show him what the danger is.

If you need to take something away from your toddler and not let him or her use it, offer something to replace it, but always with something new or interesting. In most cases, the conflict can be avoided.

It is advisable for adults involved in the upbringing of a child to discuss the limits allowed so that, as the toddler grows, he or she will not be confused: if dad considers this acceptable, why does grandma forbid it?

But do not do this in the presence of the toddler. And even when being guided by safety considerations, do not forbid several things to the child all in a row. This can destroy the child's desire for initiative or cause them excessive nervousness.

A child's desire to touch something with his hands or to taste it isn't always due to mischief (as sometimes it seems to parents). This is the normal desire that a child has to know the world around him and to gain their own experience of things.

If you treat a child with respect, you can find many ways to manage his or her behavior. But, although you cannot do without verbal correction, you should not criticize their personality. Instead, focus on the act itself.

Try not to say to a child: "You are bad!" Instead say: "You did a bad thing!" Even if your toddler does not understand everything, your attitude towards him and your tone of voice can make clear the meaning of what is happening.

Analyze the reasons for the conflicts that arise: is it possible that you are annoyed by seeing in your child a character trait that you have been trying to get rid of yourself for a long time?

When children are happy with everything, they usually behave well, but sometimes they unconsciously want to push the limits. At this time, it seems to parents that the child is testing their patience.

Often, bad behavior is a way to attract attention. The child may try to establish himself as being in opposition to the adults with whom he constantly communicates. If you see the child is very enthusiastic in an activity, try not to interrupt it, even if it's time to eat or sleep.

Help them finish their "business," and then offer whatever is needed. The child will get used to finishing what he is doing.

The most sensible way to resist hysterics and fits, if they become habitual, is to ignore them. Stay calm and kind with your child, but firmly insist on your authority and in the end your toddler will understand that lying on the floor in hysterics is not the best way to win an argument.

It is not necessary to send a child to another room, especially if you are not sure about their safety. Go about your affairs, discuss other problems with your loved ones, and let the toddler remain in your field of vision. If, after some time, the child is ready for dialogue, don't reproach him for what took place a few minutes ago.

Sometimes a child needs some help to stop the hysteria.

Each family has its own ways of settling disobedience, based on their previous experience of communicating with the child.

Try to be guided by these principles:

A child is a full member of the family (but not the center of it).

The child has the right to his own opinion (even if your toddler does not speak yet) - and this should be taken into account.

Just like an adult, the child has the right to a bad mood: from time to time they may be angry, may be dissatisfied, or may cry. It is not always because of external circumstances.

Chapter 21: Important Emergency Items To Include When Traveling By Rv With Your Baby

Traveling by RV can be one of the best possible ways to travel with a baby. Everyone has dealt with the frustration of traveling down the road in a car with a screaming baby in the backseat; beyond your reach so that you cannot take care of their basics needs without twisting yourself up like a pretzel and putting your own safety in peril. An RV can solve a multitude of travel problems and make for a vacation everyone can enjoy. However, one must consider emergency preparedness in the event of a problem during their travels. For example, it is essential to bring along important contact numbers and emergency items that can make the difference between a minor inconvenience and a major medical emergency.

One great thing about traveling by RV is that you have your home away from home with you at all times. Instead of changing your baby in a smelly gas station rest room, you can have everything within reach. One simple stop at a rest area and you can take your baby out of a car seat and manage a diaper change in a clean, safe environment. Remember to bring along anything that could help with skin disturbances during your vacation. Considering that your baby's schedule and diet may be slightly altered during your vacation, you may want to include items for skin care that you don't normally need. Even if your child is not prone to diaper rash, it is a good idea to come equipped with creams and ointments for this problem. Even if you are breast feeding, it is possible that your own diet will be altered during the trip which could result in diaper rash. Think ahead and set up a changing station' in your RV that is equipped with everything you need for a quick and easy diaper change.

Emergency prevention can be managed by babyproofing your RV just as you would baby proof your home. You may not think that you need to because the doors to cupboards and cabinets are harder to open to keep them from opening during travel. However, these doors can still be opened by force. Not only will it give your baby access to the contents of the cupboard, but the swift release of the cupboard door can result in a nasty knock to the head of face when a baby finally succeeds in releasing the cabinet door. Also, be sure to block stair wells and other areas where a baby can take a tumble.

In case there is a bump or bruise, make sure that you come equipped with the same first aid you would keep in your own home. You can purchase kits that are helpful or set one up yourself. It will probably be less expensive to make your own and you can customize it for your own family. If you also have older children, you may need to load up on the bandages and bug bite ointment! Make sure to include any medicine you may need including pain relievers, allergy medication, nasal sprays, etc. for the proper age of your baby and children. Remember that appropriate sun screen can make the difference between a good vacation and miserable children!

The most important consideration is the need for proper communication. Be absolutely sure to bring along important contact numbers in case of an emergency. For example, have a handy list with your child's pediatrician's number as well as any specialists. You want your child's medical records to be easily accessed in case something goes wrong. With proper care and prevention, the odds are that you will have no need for this list, but you should cover all bases and keep the list where anyone in the family can find it rapidly if necessary. Also, do your homework to make sure that you have access to medical help at all times before you leave for your trip. Check your cell phone coverage for the areas where you will be traveling. The last thing you want is to have a medical emergency outside of your cell phone range. If you find that your coverage is not adequate for the areas where you will be going, consider buying a cheap track phone with a carrier that is more prominent in that area so that you are always able to contact emergency help.

It may also be a good idea to map out local hospitals and urgent care clinics for the route you will be traveling. Whether a medical concern arises for the baby or another family member, it is a good idea to know where you can access help quickly. If you are going to be in an area where hospitals and urgent care clinics are not available for miles, you can call ahead and speak with someone in the local government offices to determine how they manage health emergencies.

The biggest thing you can do to ensure your child's safety during an RV trip is to provide an adequate child restraint car seat that is age appropriate and fastened to the best available place in the RV. This can be a challenge since there are many seating areas that are not designed to accommodate a car seat. Be sure to follow the instructions for safely using the car seat. For example, if you have a car seat that is designed to be rear facing, don't improvise and put it sideways. Also, be sure that any chair used for the car seat is properly affixed to the structure of the vehicle. Sometimes people will add on furniture that is not solid or properly braced. Putting a car seat in this location could lead to an extremely unsafe situation. Even a very abrupt stop could cause unsupported furniture to move about the interior of the vehicle.

You will be able to relax and enjoy your vacation knowing that you took every precaution and brought along important contact numbers and emergency items to keep your family safe and healthy during your RV vacation.

Thanks for reading. Wishing you happy and safe travels!

Chapter 22: Single Mom Child Care

Options - Baby Sitter Or Day Care

To the single mom, finding good, reliable child care can be agonizing ordeal - especially if the child is still an infant or toddler. It becomes gloomier if she has inflexible working hours. At any rate, the single mom has to provide for child care when she goes to work and basically she has only two child care options to choose from – day care or a baby sitter.

Both child care options have their strengths and weaknesses and your decision whether to choose a babysitter or a daycare center will depend on your personal preference and your personal circumstance.

Day care may cost you a lot of money. They are expensive. But if cost is not a problem then day care is the better alternative for your kid as it will give him opportunities to socialize and interact with other kids his age. Unfortunately, they have fixed operating hours which means if your work requires you to come in early and/or go home late, it may not be the best option for you.

On the other hand, getting a baby sitter affords you greater flexibility since you can just phone in if you have to come home late. Besides, you have the option to hire a baby sitter on a full time basis or only when you need one. Besides, the baby sitter can give your toddler a more focused attention than what he can get in a child care center.

The only problem with hiring a baby sitter you can never be 100% sure that your kid is getting the kind of care and attention promised since you are not there to observe it. Often, you get to find out that the sitter you hired is lacking in skills or has issues that affect her work as a caregiver only after you've hired her.

To ensure that you have the most qualified candidate for the job, you should spend time to thoroughly investigate the qualifications and backgrounds of each candidate. You also have to check on their references to make sure they are who they claim they are and they can provide the kind of care you expect them to give your child.

To help you out in your search for the perfect baby sitter, here is a list of questions you should ask your potential hires.

Ask the candidate to detail her care giving experiences particularly her baby sitting experiences with kids of the same age as yours. Make her relate to you her most challenging experience as a baby sitter and how she managed the incident.

Ask her for character references and past babysitting jobs and make sure she gives you the complete names, addresses, and phone numbers. Call everyone in the list and get as much information as you can about her from these people.

Ask about her availability and working schedule. Find out if she can accommodate a flexible schedule to fit your specific needs if and when the situation calls for it.

Ask if she has undergone first aid training or any other training that qualifies her to give emergency care to a child.

Find out about her perspective on handling unruly behavior and what she thinks about giving punishments to kids for misbehaving.

Ask her if she has her own means of transportation going to work and coming home from work.

Give her several sticky child care scenarios and ask her how she would handle each one of them.

Ask her what pay rate she is expecting.

Find out if she is legally authorized to work in the U.S.

Be thorough in your investigation so you can have peace of mind when you leave your kid with your hired baby sitter. Don't go rushing in to hire a candidate just because she strikes you as responsible and caring enough. Always double check the references.

Chapter 23: Work On Yourself

.You have to improve yourself. Just about all parents want their kids to get better throughout life. If you expect your kids to get better then you should apply the same thought process to yourself. Children will improve if you as a parent model that growth for them.

Take The Responsibility (No blame game or justifying)

This may be my biggest annoyance and it is when parents never take responsibility for their kids. Along with that parents that never hold their kids responsible for their actions. It just seems to always be someone else's fault or ADHD's fault. It is either the principal, teacher, or the whole school's fault but never your fault or your child's fault. Often times these parents can point out the flaws in other parents, teachers and administrators so well while missing their own. Reminds me of an analogy from the Bible that says:

"Why do you see the speck that is in your brother's eye, but do not notice the log that is in your own eye? Or how can you say to your brother, 'Let me take the speck out of your eye,' when there is the log in your own eye? You hypocrite, first take the log out of your own eye, and then you will see clearly to take the speck out of your brother's eye."

(Matthew 7:3-5)

You have to stop worrying about the problem in other people and make sure you are taking care of your kids and your own issues first. Sometimes I am appalled at parents' reactions when they are called because of their child's misbehavior. I can vividly remember a call going home for a child who was talking out loud to herself during the test after repeatedly given nonverbal and verbal warnings to stop. After the situation was explained to this child's mother, her response was "she couldn't have been the only one talking, you just picking on my daughter". Then she hung up the phone. This is a HUGE problem! You are teaching your kid that it is ok to do wrong because you are going to take their side and shift blame onto someone else. Everything you do now as a parent affects the future of your child.

Let's fast forward some years when your child is associating with friends who are not good influences because they've been taught to shift blame on others. They believe even though they hang out with bad influences they can blame their way out of any situation. They are in high school driving a car and pulled over by a cop. The cop proceeds to search the car and finds drugs under the passenger seat that your child is sitting in. The friend does not admit that they are his or her drugs. Shifting blame is not going to get your child out of trouble in this situation. Your child is now guilty by association. By law this is known as "Constructive Possession" or can be charged as parties to a crime. This is real life here, so hold yourself and your kids highly responsible for their actions. My suggestion is to not even worry about anyone else's action when your child has done something wrong. Finding out the facts is important but it is not nearly as important as making sure your child behaves and responds correctly.

Kids who are not held accountable for their actions will continuously push the limits of what they can do that is wrong because they know that you as a parent will come bail them out when they mess up, then blame someone or something else for the problem. The only blame that needs to happen is to blame yourself and then make actions to help your child become better. If you do not hold your kid responsible for their actions now eventually you won't just be bailing them out of trouble at school, you will be bailing them out of trouble in jail.

Most people who achieve massive success constantly take responsibility for everything that happens to them. This mindset can be summed up in this example: if a thunderstorm happened and it knocked their power out, many high achievers would take the blame for not having a backup generator ready. The reason it is so crucial for you to take responsibility for yourself and your child is because it gives you both the opportunity to take some real control of the circumstances in your life and be able to prevent or avoid them.

My Kid Don't Act Like That At Home

School is not home! The environment is totally different. There are 20 something other kids in a room. Along with that your child is being instructed to do things that are not just fun things. Writing papers, doing classwork, and being challenged is not something that most kids would consider fun. This environment will and can cause your child to act differently than at home with you. This is why you want to train your child how to act when in public and at school. You must help them to understand that they need to be respectful and to behave just as well if you were right there with them at school. This will help give your child a better chance to learn what is being taught.

As mentioned earlier in this book you as the parent are the most important form of education that your child will receive. You must talk to them and set the tone for their approach towards school. One way to help transition kids into the school situations is to emulate a learning environment at home. This means your child is not just watching tv, playing video games, on their smartphones, or the computer but they have to sit down and focus on some work. This can be reading a book, writing an essay, painting or even some type of educational game but the purpose is to have them sit down and focus on something. This does not have to be something boring because learning can always be fun but you have to take time to make it creative. There is a variety of options for you to choose from.

Chapter 24: Staying Close To Your Daughter

The best way to raise a daughter that is healthy both inside and out is to stay close to her so she knows you are always there for her and that she can come to you when she needs to. Here are some things you can do to stay close to your daughter, even when she starts to grow up.

**You can set the time for dinner. Research has shown that children who eat with their families during dinner several times every week tend to use drugs less frequently and smoke less than if they dined alone, and are also proven to perform better in school. Since dinner is most often the time of day when the family can get together as a whole, you can try to make it a family affair. Share thoughts, talk about your day or plan weekend outings and activities while you are enjoying your daughter's company, and she will most likely do the same.

**Give your teen some space but stay close to her. It is only natural for adolescents to develop a want to spend time with their friends more than their family. However, this doesn't mean that your duties as a parent are at a minimum. To the contrary, you have to be alert at this point in your daughter's life. Do your best to find ways to stay involved in your daughter's world. Although having tea parties are something from the past, you can still meet your daughter's friends by making them feel welcomed in your home after school. Even though staying involved in your daughter's world can prove to be a challenge, it is very important in enhancing the relationship you have with her.

Don't be afraid to share your feelings with her. Telling your daughter about how you feel confused, angry, insecure or awkward will show your daughter that there's also a side of you that's human. Of course, you should spare her from the more intimate details of problems. Not only will this pave the way for you to become closer to your daughter, but you will also make it easier for her to talk to you about her own problems when these come up.

Ask what she thinks. Involve your daughter in family discussions. Especially when she turns into a teenager, she will have an opinion about everything and she won't feel shy about sharing them and telling them to you. Therefore you should allow your daughter to make decisions of her own. For example, let your daughter decide when she would like to study, what clothes she will wear, which people she should be friends with and what course she will take when she graduates from high school. However, along with this, keep in mind that there are some major decisions that are not negotiable. As a parent you still have to set limits to your child in order to protect her health and well-being, which can include decisions on curfews, sexual activities, drinking and issues regarding university life.

**Trust that your daughter will make smart choices. Although there will be times when she won't, it's always good to give confidence to what your daughter can do. Especially when they turn to legal age, you should give them the opportunity and chance to solve their own problems, just like how you would have wanted it with your parents when you were her age.

**Give your daughter some privacy. It is important that she realizes that you respect her private space. Before you enter her room, always knock first and ask politely. Don't ever go over her private possessions such her diary, eavesdrop in her conversations with friends over the phone or ask her a lot of questions. If she has a behavior that troubles you, ask her directly about it and address it by using the words "can we talk about it?".

**Be honest with what you feel towards your daughter's actions. A lot of parents nowadays make the mistake of offering praise when it isn't appropriate or necessary, as well as when they should not, which only undermines trust. If your daughter learns that both your criticisms and praises are valid and honest, she will learn to give you her trust.

**Finally, be involved with your daughter's interests. If she is someone who likes to play tennis, offer coaching or simply watch her during practice or whenever she is competing. If she takes piano lessons, go to her recitals and listen to her practice. Give positive feedback on how much efforts she puts into her hobbies, interests and diversions. Study up in her interests so you can talk about it with her and help her improve.

Conclusion

Thank you again for downloading this book!

I hope this book was able to help you to learn techniques for creating a positive and trusting environment for your children.

The next step is to start working with your kids to create a more positive home.

Thank you and good luck!

www.ingramcontent.com/pod-product-compliance
Lightning Source LLC
Chambersburg PA
CBHW072003070526
44583CB00015B/1305